Sales promotion law
A practical guide

To Gaenor,
for putting up with all my eccentricities.

Sales promotion law
A practical guide

Philip Circus, BA(Law), MPhil, DCA, Barrister

Consultant Legal Adviser, Institute of Sales Promotion
Legal Affairs Director, Institute of Practitioners in Advertising
Marketing law consultant

Butterworths
London, Dublin & Edinburgh
1995

United Kingdom	Butterworths, a Division of Reed Elsevier (UK) Ltd, Halsbury House, 35 Chancery Lane, LONDON WC2A 1EL and 4 Hill Street EDINBURGH EH2 3JZ
Australia	Butterworths, SYDNEY, MELBOURNE, BRISBANE, ADELAIDE, PERTH, CANBERRA and HOBART
Canada	Butterworths Canada Ltd, TORONTO and VANCOUVER
Ireland	Butterworth (Ireland) Ltd, DUBLIN
Malaysia	Malayan Law Journal Sdn Bhd, KUALA LUMPUR
New Zealand	Butterworths of New Zealand Ltd, WELLINGTON and AUCKLAND
Puerto Rico	Butterworth of Puerto Rico, Inc, SAN JUAN
Singapore	Butteworths Asia, SINGAPORE
South Africa	Butterworths Publishers (Pty) Ltd, DURBAN
USA	Butterworth Legal Publishers, CARLSBAD, California and SALEM, New Hampshire

All rights reserved. No part of this publication may be reproduced in any material form (including photocopying or storing it in any medium by electronic means and whether or not transiently or incidentally to some other use of this publication) without the written permission of the copyright owner except in accordance with the provisions of the Copyright, Designs and Patents Act 1988 or under the terms of a licence issued by the Copyright Licensing Agency Ltd, 90 Tottenham Court Road, London, England W1P 9HE. Applications for the copyright owner's written permission to reproduce any part of this publication should be addressed to the publisher.

Warning: The doing of an unauthorised act in relation to a copyright work may result in both a civil claim for damages and criminal prosecution.

© Reed Elsevier (UK) Ltd 1995

A CIP Catalogue record for this book is available from the British Library.

ISBN 0 406 04803 7

Typeset by Grahame & Grahame Editorial, Brighton
Printed by Clays Ltd, St Ives plc

PREFACE

It is unusual for a book on marketing law to exhaust its print run, thus necessitating a second edition. That this book has done so has vindicated the novel approach we took in 1989, when Tony Painter and I created the first edition. What we wanted to achieve was a truly user-friendly book for the many non-lawyers who need a guide to sales promotion law.

From the comments I have received from the industry, the question and answer approach has worked well because it has targeted the everyday questions that are asked by practitioners. In my experience, sales promotion is the most commercially responsive of the marketing disciplines. It has to be because it is at the sharp end of shifting goods and services. That sales promotion practitioners should have reacted so favourably to this book has given me enormous professional satisfaction. I hope my readers will find this new edition a worthy successor.

I am indebted to many people who have helped me on my way. Tony Painter, with whom I created the first edition, has kindly allowed me generous use of his original material. Sue Short of the Institute of Sales Promotion continues to be a stalwart supporter of this book, and much of the advice in it has been honed through many a discussion with her on sales promotion problems.

I am grateful to Charles Swan of The Simkins Partnership, who not only read through the draft of my chapter on intellectual property, but also convinced me that I knew more about intellectual property than I thought I did. Gratitude also goes to my friend and colleague, Alan White, a former chief trading standards officer, who gave me advice on some aspects of weights and measures legislation and unit pricing.

The IPA, and Nick Phillips, its Director General, have been a constant support in my endeavours. It was in advising IPA members about sales promotion schemes that I first developed a knowledge and interest in sales promotion law.

Other organisations have helped willingly by allowing me to reproduce their codes of practice, in particular the Chartered Institute of Purchasing and Supply, the Incorporated Society of British Advertisers and the Committee of Advertising Practice.

I owe a particular debt of gratitude to the many people in the sales promotion and advertising industries who in presenting me with their problems have helped develop my understanding of this fascinating area of law.

Finally, a big thank you to Melanie Laroche, my loyal and long-suffering secretary. Without her patient handling of my scribbles this book would never have been possible.

Philip Circus

London, April 1995

CONTENTS

Preface   v

Chapter 1   The legal and self-regulatory controls on sales promotion   1
   Legal controls 1
   Civil law 2
   Criminal law 2
   Codes of practice 4
   Self-regulation 5
   Other bodies 9
   Television and radio 10

Chapter 2   Contractual issues   11
   The nature of contracts 11
   Fulfilment of promotions 12
   Limitations on offers 13
   Extension of offers 14
   General disclaimers 14
   Delivery 15
   Terms of the offer 15
   Refunds 16
   Misdescription of goods 16
   Criminal law and failure to fulfil offers 17
   Quality of promotional goods 18
   The quality of services 19
   Suitability of promotional products 20
   Unsolicited goods and services 20
   Limited editions 21
   Identity of the promoter 22

Chapter 3   Prize draws   24
   Lotteries legislation 24
   Contribution 25
   Newspaper, bingo and 'instant win' 28
   Telephone calls and postage 30
   Prosecutions 31
   Prizes 32

Chapter 4   Competitions   33
Definition 33
Illegal competitions 33
Multi-stage schemes 35
Particular types of competition 36
Contractual issues 37
Competition rules 38
Changing the goal posts 40
Publicity 41

Chapter 5   Intellectual property   42
Definitions 42
Ownership of copyright 43
Ideas and concepts 44
Moral rights 45
Practical issues 46
Trade marks 47
Patents 49

Chapter 6   Price promotions   51
Indications that a price is less than it actually is 51
Reductions from a previous price 52
Recommended prices 55
Introductory offers 57
Comparisons with other traders' prices 58
References to value or worth 60
Sales and special events 60
Price comparisons in different circumstances 61
Post and packing etc charges 63
VAT 63
Mail order trade 64
Newspaper and magazine advertisements 64
Other price indications 64
Vouchers and coupons 65

Chapter 7   Free and extra value incentives   67
Free offers 67
Extra value packs 70
Multiple packs 72

Chapter 8   Mail order and direct marketing promotions   74
Some general rules about mailed promotions 74
Unsolicited promotional goods 76
Trading lists 78

Chapter 9 Bribery and corruption 80
  Lessening the risk 83
  Rules and guidance 83
  Prosecutions 84
  Sales Promotion Code 84
  Tax 85

Chapter 10 Miscellaneous legal issues 86
  Trading Stamps 86
  The safety of promotional goods 88
  Consumer credit 89
  Origin making 91
  Companies Act 1985 91
  Other legislation 92
  Charity promotions 93

Chapter 11 Europe 96
  Background 96
  Commission involvement in marketing 99
  European legislation 100
  Cassis de Dijon 101
  The European sales promotion scene 102
  European self-regulation 103

Chapter 12 Administration checklist 105

Appendices 111
  1 The British Codes of Advertising and Sales Promotion 113
  2 The Code of Practice for Traders on Price Indications 168
  3 Notes for Guidance on Coupons – Recommended Best Practice 191
  4 The Institute of Sales Promotion: Promotional Handling Code of Practice 198
  5 Incorporated Society of British Advertisers: Trade Incentives – Good and Bad Practice 211
  6 The Chartered Institute of Purchasing and Supply: Ethical Code 214
  7 The Chartered Institute of Purchasing and Supply: Rules for Trade Promotions 217
  8 Checklist of restrictions on sales promotion activities in individual countries 219
  9 Useful addresses 222

Index 225

CHAPTER 1

THE LEGAL AND SELF-REGULATORY CONTROLS ON SALES PROMOTION

Legal controls

Question: What do we mean by sales promotion law?

Answer: People talk about sales promotion law as if it were a coherent body of law in its own right. However, this is not so since it is doubtful if the Parliamentary Counsel, the drafters of legislation, have even heard of the term 'sales promotion', let alone understand what it is and how it operates. Accordingly, when we talk of sales promotion law what we mean is that collection of laws which has an effect, often an individual one and sometimes an unintended one, on sales promotion.

Question: When we talk about law, what do we actually mean?

Answer: The law can be sub-divided into a number of categories and these we consider in subsequent questions. One significant characteristic of the law is its comprehensiveness of application, unlike self-regulation for example, which generally only applies to members of an association. The main distinction is between civil law and criminal law.

2 The legal and self-regulatory controls on sales promotion

Civil law

Question: What is civil law?

Answer: Civil law is designed to assist individuals in enforcing what are essentially individual rights, for example trespass, defamation or breach of contract. The point is that society as a whole is not involved, since the object of civil law is compensation for individual wrong rather than punishment.

Question: What courts are relevant to civil law matters?

Answer: Minor matters are dealt with by the county courts and within the county courts there is provision for what are termed 'small claims' – invariably those consumer complaints which, although they raise important issues, nevertheless relate to relatively small sums of money. Cases can go to arbitration within the county court system and this does much to overcome some of the fear that people have of litigation. More serious matters are dealt with at the High Court. Avenues of appeal lie to the Court of Appeal (Civil Division) and the House of Lords.

Criminal law

Question: What then is the position of the criminal law?

Answer: Criminal law deals with those wrongs which are considered to be more than just a question of individual rights. Accordingly, the State, in its various guises, is the initiator of the action and the objective is not compensation but the punishment and supression of crime. Having said that, increasingly the criminal courts are making use of section 35 of the Powers of Criminal Courts Act 1973 to award compensation to those who have suffered loss as a result of crime.

Question: Who then enforces the criminal law that is relevant to sales promotion?

Answer: Most consumer protection law is enforced by trading standards officers who are local government employees. Such areas as consumer credit and the law on price indications are enforced by trading standards departments. An element of co-ordination of policy amongst the many trading standards departments is achieved through the Local Authorities Co-ordinating Body on Food and Trading Standards (LACOTS). The police are responsible for enforcing the law relating to lotteries and competitions, and bribery and corruption.

Question: What courts are relevant to the enforcement of the criminal law?

Answer: Most criminal cases are dealt with in the magistrates' courts. Some are tried there because they are called summary offences, which can only be dealt with by magistrates. Many more are dealt with there out of choice by the defendants. This is because defendants often have a choice of trial by magistrates or trial by jury at the Crown Court. Rarely do defendants choose the latter because of the time, expense and the potentially greater sentence that can be awarded against them. Appeal from a decision of the magistrates can go either to the Crown Court or, on a point of law, to the Divisional Court of the High Court. Further appeals are possible to the Court of Appeal (Criminal Division) and the House of Lords.

Question: People sometimes talk about case law and sometimes about statutes. What is the difference?

Answer: Unlike many continental countries, the basis of English law has been the decisions of the judges over the centuries in making precedents which are followed in later cases. This is what we mean by the term 'common law'. Large parts of the law, both criminal and civil, are rooted in the common law. For example, although the law establishes the penalties for murder, the definition of murder is laid down by the common law and not by an act of Parliament. Statute law is the law which has emanated from Parliament through either acts of Parliament or through statutory instruments, which are made by ministers under the authority given to them by acts of Parliament. Statute law is increasingly important, particularly because the doctrine of judicial precedent means that decisions of judges are binding unless overruled by a higher court. As society has developed and as changes have taken place, Parliament has been seen as a far quicker way of changing the law than leaving changes to the judges. However, that does not mean that individual case decisions are not important. As we look at particular areas of sales promotion law we shall note some highly crucial court decisions.

Codes of practice

Question: What of codes of practice?

Answer: Codes of practice seem to be very popular these days and there are an enormous number of them. They vary enormously in their status, scope and effectiveness. Broadly speaking we can divide codes of practice into two categories: statutory codes and self-regulatory ones.

Question: What are statutory codes?

Answer: There are many different types of statutory code, but what they all have in common is that their creation is invariably sanctioned by an act of Parliament. Frequently, compliance with the code will be taken into consideration in deciding whether the Act's requirements have been met. The best example is the Highway Code. Although compliance with the

Code is not a legal requirement, it will be taken into account in deciding whether an offence has been committed. For example, the Code says that one should look in the mirror before pulling away from the kerb. Failure to do so is not a criminal offence but if, as a result of not looking in the mirror, one has an accident which results in a prosecution for careless driving, then failure to follow the Code will be taken into consideration in deciding whether an offence has taken place. In sales promotion, the best example of a statutory code is the Code of Practice for Traders on Price Indications, issued under Section 25 of the Consumer Protection Act 1987. This we look at further in Chapter 6.

Self-regulation

Question: What are self-regulatory codes?

Answer: These are non-governmental codes, usually issued by a trade association in order to establish and maintain certain standards for members to follow. Section 124(3) of the Fair Trading Act 1973 imposes on the Director General of Fair Trading (DGFT) the duty to encourage the creation and dissemination of such codes. There are over twenty such codes, ranging from footwear and double glazing to telecommunications services.

Question: Where does the Advertising Standards Authority fit into all this?

Answer: The Advertising Standards Authority (ASA) was founded in 1962 as a separate body with an independent chairman and a majority of members independent of the business, to oversee the British self-regulatory system of advertising control. The system covers all non-broadcast advertising, except cable advertising which is the responsibility of the Independent Television Commission. The ASA is the public face of advertising self-regulation and deals with all complaints concerning alleged breaches of the British Code of Advertising Practice and the Code of Sales Promotion Practice. The ASA is funded by an automatic 0.1% levy on all display advertising, which is collected by the Advertising Standards Board of Finance (ASBOF).

Question: What then is CAP?

Answer: CAP is the colloquial way of referring to the Committee of Advertising Practice, which is the industry element in the system of advertising control. Made up of representatives of the various associations which support the self-regulatory system, its chief responsibilities are the preparation and review of the two codes of practice.

Question: What are the codes that CAP is responsible for drafting and keeping under review?

Answer: The British Code of Advertising and the British Code of Sales Promotion. Since January 1995 these Codes have been published in one volume. Compliance with the Sales Promotion Code will seem obvious but it is also important to comply with the British Code of Advertising as this will frequently have a relevance to sales promotion schemes. For example, the provisions on mail order may be particularly relevant, as well as the Code's provisions on list and database practice. The mail order provisions of the Advertising Code are discussed in detail in Chapter 8.

Question: Tell me more about the Sales Promotion Code.

Answer: The British Code of Sales Promotion was first published in 1974, and the latest edition is 1995. As to the scope of the Code one could not do better than quote General Rules two and three from the Code:

'2. The Sales Promotion Code is designed primarily to protect the public but it also applies to trade promotions and incentive schemes and to the promotional elements of sponsorships.

3. The Sales Promotion Code regulates the nature and administration of promotional marketing techniques. These techniques generally involve providing a range of direct or indirect additional benefits, usually on a temporary basis, designed to make goods or services more attractive to purchasers.'

Question: How is the Code organised?

Answer: The Code is divided into a number of sections. After an introduction the Code's basic principles are set out. There then follows general guidelines applying to all forms of sales promotion, as well as rules relating to particular cases. A helpful listing of the main legislative controls is set out at the end of the two Codes.

The Sales Promotion Code is set out in full in Appendix 1, together with the Advertising Code.

Question: What are the sanctions of the self-regulatory system?

Answer: The main sanction is publicity, which is achieved through the ASA and CAP case reports. These receive a wide distribution amongst the press, television, government departments etc. The ASA also issues media notices which advise the media proprietors of breaches of the Code. This information is useful to publishers in exercising their discretion as to whether or not to reject advertisement copy – a right which media proprietors have long cherished and which was judicially recognised in the case of *Gamage (A W) Ltd v Temple Press Ltd* (1911).

In addition, the associations which support the self-regulatory system make it a requirement of membership that members will comply with the codes of practice and with the rulings of the ASA and CAP.

Question: If I don't like a ruling from the ASA is there anything that can be done about it?

Answer: There is no formal channel of appeal from an ASA decision but before the ASA Council make their decision one can ask for a case to go before the CAP General Media Review Panel, where the matter will get the consideration of advertising practitioners.

Question: What happens if someone is unaffected by the available sanctions, and decides to ignore the ASA's rulings?

Answer: In cases of misleading advertising – a term which is defined very widely – the Director-General of Fair Trading (DGFT) has powers under the Control of Misleading Advertisements Regulations 1988 to secure court orders banning 'misleading advertisements' – a term which covers sales promotions as well. The DGFT is empowered to refer complainants to what are termed 'established means', which for our purposes will usually be either the trading standards service or the ASA. It is only a tiny number of cases which call for the powers of the DGFT and these usually arise where the ASA either cannot act, or cannot act quickly enough.

Question: Can I get advice from CAP?

Answer: Yes. CAP as the industry part of the self-regulatory system offers a comprehensive, free advisory service on copy.

Other bodies

Question: We have heard about ICSTIS. Does that have a relevance to sales promotion?

Answer: ICSTIS (the Independent Committee for the Supervision of Standards of Telephone Information Services) was set up in September 1986, following extreme criticism of the use of some forms of commercial exploitation of premium rate telephone lines – especially in respect of sexually-orientated services. The Committee is an independent watchdog, funded by the telephone companies, to supervise premium or special rate telephone information and entertainment services. It has the power to fine and the power to ban a company from use of the network for a breach of its Code of Practice

The ICSTIS Code has a section on sales promotion which should be carefully considered, if a promotion is to make use of a special rate 'phone facility. In particular, the Code requires the rates for a premium rate number to be set out clearly. It is also worth bearing in mind that ICSTIS, like CAP, offers advice on copy clearance.

Question: What other industry bodies have rules or guidance which are relevant to sales promotion?

Answer: The Institute of Sales Promotion has issued two documents of interest to the sales promotion world. These are the 'Notes for Guidance on Coupons' and the 'Promotional Handling Code of Practice' – the latter being a code of practice for handling houses. Both of these documents are set out as appendices. The Chartered Institute of Purchasing and Supply has issued 'Rules for Trade Promotions' which we touch on in Chapter 9, on bribery and corruption. This document is also set out as an appendix.

10 The legal and self-regulatory controls on sales promotion
Television and radio

Question: Where does the ITC fit into all this?

Answer: The Independent Television Commission (ITC) is the statutory body responsible for the control of television and radio advertising. It is required under the Broadcasting Act 1990 to establish a code of practice for television advertising and to see that it is complied with. In practice most of the spade work in clearing television commercials is carried out by the Broadcast Advertising Clearance Centre (BACC) on behalf of the television companies.

Question: Are the ITC rules relevant to sales promotion?

Answer: All television advertising, and that includes advertising of promotions, must comply with the ITC Code. There are some specific rules which have a bearing on sales promotion. For example, in relation to medicines, rule 24 in Appendix 3 says that advertisements shall not contain any reference to a prize competition or similar scheme. In relation to alcohol, to take another example, rule 39(L) provides that no advertisement for alcoholic drinks may publicise competitions or other sales promotion which entail or encourage multiple purchase.

Question: What about the Radio Authority?

Answer: The Broadcasting Act 1990 established, in addition to the ITC, a new statutory authority for the regulation of commercial radio. The Radio Authority (RA) establishes a Code of Practice to which radio advertisements must comply.

CHAPTER 2

CONTRACTUAL ISSUES

The nature of contracts

Question: What do we mean by a contract?

Answer: For there to be a contract there needs to be three elements present – an offer and acceptance, consideration, and an intention to create legal relations.

Question: What do these terms means?

Answer:
(a) *Offer and acceptance:* This means that there must be a clear and definite agreement between both parties, analysed in terms of a definite offer or proposition from one party and a clear unequivocal acceptance from the other.

(b) *Consideration:* Every contract must have the presence of consideration. In *Currie v Misa* (1875), it was held that consideration 'may consist either in some right, interest, profit, or benefit accruing to the one party, or some forbearance, detriment, loss or responsibility given, suffered, or undertaken by the other'.

An illustration helps. If one party agrees with another to sell them their car for £5,000 there will be consideration and a contract. If one party agrees to give the car away as a gift, there is no consideration and no contract. One important rule is that consideration does not have to be adequate or reasonable – simply that it has value.

(c) *Intention to create legal relations:* This simply

Contractual issues

means that the parties must intend their agreement to give rise to legal implications. An agreement between a husband and wife will usually not give rise to such an intention, whereas an agreement between business people invariably will.

Question: What is the contractual position when we run a promotion?

Answer: The offer of goods or services with incentives and the acceptance of that offer by a consumer is an enforceable contract and any breach of the terms, conditions or nature of the offer is actionable by the consumer. So too are agreements between sales promotion consultancies and their clients, between promoters and sourcing agencies, and the many other agreements necessary to run a promotion.

Question: What about the terms of the contract?

Answer: There are two main types of contractual term – express and implied. The express terms are those stated expressly in a written contract, in written terms of business and sometimes in correspondence where they are leading up to the contract and the parties intend to be bound by them.

Courts are reluctant to imply terms into a contract, but will do so when it is necessary to give effect to the presumed intention of the parties or to reflect custom and practice in the trade.

Fulfilment of promotions

Question: We have offered a free set of place mats with our usual range of canteens of cutlery. Due to unexpected demand we have run out of the place mats before the expiry date of the offer. Can we offer different place mats or a price reduction instead?

Answer: This depends on the terms of the offer. If you offered specific place mats up to a definite termination date then you have a binding contract with any buyer who takes advantage of the offer and you cannot offer other goods or a price reduction in lieu of the place mats. On the other hand, if your promotional literature made it clear that other goods of equivalent value or a price reduction of that value would be given if stocks ran out you have no problem. These alternatives must be made clear in the original promotion. You cannot change the terms of the offer at a later date after you realise that you have insufficient stocks. The Sales Promotion Code (the Code) requires that a genuine attempt should be made to anticipate demand but in circumstances in which an unexpectedly high level of demand leads to an inability to supply, contingency plans should be made to provide unsuccessful applicants with some similar alternative of equivalent or greater value, either in cash or in kind; and the promoter's intention to act thus should be made clear to consumers before they are committed to participation. 'Equivalent value' should be assessed in terms of consumers' likely perceptions of quality and price or cost.

Limitations on offers

Question: What limitations can be placed on an offer of promotional goods other than an expiry date?

Answer: Bearing in mind what we have said above, the normal method of closing an offer is to print 'Offer closes on 21 January' etc prominently on the promotional literature and, where appropriate, on the pack. So far as the law is concerned, the offer could be limited to a specified number of applicants or 'subject to availability'. However, the Code, which seeks to prevent damage to the reputation of the industry, states that promoters are not relieved of the obligation to take all reasonable steps to avoid disappointing the consumer. This rule does not apply to the offer of genuine 'limited editions' (see below).

Extension of offers

Question: If we have stocks of promotional goods left after the expiry date can we extend the period of the offer?

Answer: Yes, provided all consumers who have applied before the closing date have received their goods and the new extended closing date is clearly stated on all promotional material.

General disclaimers

Question: Can we use words such as 'no refunds can be given if promotional goods are out of stock or are unacceptable'?

Answer: The rights of consumers to reject goods or services which do not conform to a reasonable standard of quality is enshrined in law and cannot be taken away. In addition, it is a criminal offence to exhibit or state a disclaimer which seeks to limit or remove the consumer's rights.

It is not of itself unlawful to try to limit liability where goods cannot be delivered but such a disclaimer will only be effective in so far as it is 'reasonable'. What is 'unreasonable' must be determined on the facts of each case but given that the Code frowns on any activity which would lead to consumer disappointment it is likely that a court would rule that such a disclaimer is unreasonable and therefore of no effect.

Delivery

Question: What is the maximum period of delivery of incentive goods after receipt of an application from a consumer?

Answer: There is no specified period in law. Delivery must be within a reasonable period bearing in mind the nature and cost of the goods and the type of promotion involved. However, the Code requires delivery to be within 28 days of application except where the nature of the products concerned makes it impracticable. The Code rule should be adhered to except where it is impracticable in which case an indication of the different delivery period should be stated in the promotional literature.

Terms of the offer

Question: We wish to make an 'on-pack' offer for free additional goods. What information must appear on the outside of the pack and what can we put on the inside?

Answer: By law the terms of an offer should be clear, unambiguous and easy to understand. If they are not then the contract may be enforced in favour of the consumer. The Code requires that all information which might reasonably affect a consumer's decision to buy must be given before the decision to buy is made. In particular any terms or conditions which exclude some consumers from the opportunity to participate in the promotion; impose any geographical limits on eligibility or limits on the number of applications permitted; limit the number of promotional products or prizes which an individual or household may claim or win; require additional proofs of purchase; or impose a closing date should be given particular prominence.

16 Contractual issues

Refunds

Question: Are we under an obligation to refund the purchase price of the principal product when the incentive product is faulty?

Answer: Yes. There is a single contract for the supply of the substantive and promotional products which can be repudiated by the consumer if either should be faulty. The Code requires that promoters should ensure that faulty goods are replaced without delay or that the consumer receives an immediate refund. Where payment has been made by the consumer the alternative of an exchange of goods cannot be insisted upon.

Misdescription of goods

Question: What are the liabilities of promoters if incentive goods are accidentally misdescribed?

Answer: If the goods do not conform to any description of them the consumer has a right to reject them and have his or her money back. If the description is false to a material degree an offence against the Trade Descriptions Act 1968 may have been committed. This Act creates offences of strict liability and it is no defence that the misdescription is accidental.

Question: Are there any rules about the presentation of promotional information?

Answer: It is implicit in the Code that all necessary promotional information is presented in a manner which is easy to understand and not misleading. So far as the law is concerned information which, although complete in itself, is confusing, would be likely to render a contract unenforceable. More important perhaps, is the judgment in *Read Bros Cycles (Leyton) Ltd v Waltham Forest London Borough Council* (1978) where all the information necessary for consumers to understand the offer was given, but it was split between advertisements and notices and was generally confusing. The court held that an offence concerning a misleading indication of price (see chapter 6) was committed.

Criminal law and failure to fulfil offers

Question: Is it an offence against the Trade Descriptions Act 1968 if the offer of incentive goods or services is not fulfilled?

Answer: Generally speaking there is no offence in criminal law where incentive goods are offered but not supplied. The enforcement authorities have unsuccessfully attempted to employ section 14(1)(b) of the Trade Descriptions Act 1968 to prosecute cases where this has happened. That offence concerns the reckless making of a statement which is false as to the provision of a service. In *Kinchin v Ashton Park Scooters Ltd* (1984), for example, it was held that the failure to provide free gifts offered on the purchase of a motor scooter was outside the scope of the Act. Again, in *Dixons Ltd v Roberts* (1984) it was held that failure to provide a refund claimed in consequence of an advertised offer of 'refund the difference if you buy Dixon's Deal products cheaper locally at any time of purchase and call within seven days' was not an offence against the Act. Similarly, in *Newell and Taylor v Hicks* (1983) it was held that failure to provide free video recorders with every purchase of a car was not an offence. However, in *Warwickshire County Council v Dixons* (1993), it was held that a failure to honour a price promise can give rise to liability for a misleading price indication under part III of the Consumer Protection Act 1987.

18 Contractual issues

It should be borne in mind that all of these cases would have been actionable at civil law, even where there is no criminal liability, and all, of course, are breaches of the Code.

Quality of promotional goods

Question: Are there any requirements as to the quality of promotional goods?

Answer: In all sales of goods there is an implied term about quality by virtue of the Sale and Supply of Goods Act 1994.

Under section 1 of the Act, where the seller sells goods in the course of business, there is an implied term that the goods are of satisfactory quality. 'Satisfactory quality' is defined as goods meeting the standard that a reasonable person would regard as satisfactory – taking into account the description, the price and all other relevant circumstances.

The Sale and Supply of Goods Act 1994, being new legislation, is yet to be tested in the courts. However, the Act says that the quality of goods includes their state and condition of the goods, and gives examples of factors which, in appropriate cases, can be regarded as aspects of the quality of goods:

(a) fitness for all the purposes for which goods of the kind in question are commonly supplied;

(b) appearance and finish;

(c) freedom from minor defects;

(d) safety; and

(e) durability.

If these conditions of contract are not fulfilled the buyer may reject the goods within a reasonable period after purchase and ask for his or her money back. Any offer of an exchange of goods or credit notes may be accepted at the discretion of the buyer and cannot be insisted upon.

It should always be remembered that non-conformity with description may also be a criminal offence under the Trade Descriptions Act 1968.

The Code requires that all promotional products meet satisfactory standards of safety, durability and performance in use. When applicable, such matters as guarantees and the availability of servicing should be clearly explained.

The quality of services

Question: Where offers such as 'free fitting' or '12 months' free service' are made are there any requirements as to the quality of such services?

Answer: As in the case of goods above, the law imposes certain implied conditions in all consumer contracts. They are:

- the supplier will carry out the service with reasonable care and skill – the degree of care and skill is that which a reasonably competent person in the particular trade or industry could be expected to have. In such cases the promoter is liable for any defective work carried out by his own or contracted employees;

- the service must be carried out in a reasonable time – unless the contract specifies a time when the work will be carried out there is an implied term that the work will be completed within a reasonable time. What is reasonable is a question of fact in every case but in the typical 'free fitting' promotion the period will be a matter of hours or days so that the buyer can make almost immediate use of the product.

Suitability of promotional products

Question: Are there any precautions of which promoters should be aware as to sensitive products groups for consumers?

Answer: It need hardly be said that obscenity should be avoided but it is often not understood that it is unlawful to send to any person any book, magazine or leaflet which is unsolicited and which describes or illustrates human sexual techniques.

In more general terms the Code states that promoters should not offer promotional products which are of a nature likely to cause offence or products which, in the context of the promotion, may reasonably be considered to be socially undesirable. Promoters are required to take special care with promotional products, the distribution of which is subject to any form of legal restriction. Particular care should also be taken in the distribution of free samples to ensure that children or other particularly vulnerable groups are not harmed.

Unsolicited goods and services

Question: What are the constraints on sending out unsolicited incentives?

Answer: There is nothing to prevent the despatch of unsolicited incentives which are not specifically forbidden by law on grounds of taste or safety (eg explosive or flammable goods, material on sexual techniques etc). However, under the Unsolicited Goods and Services Act 1971, no payment of any kind may be demanded and there is no right to such payment provided the recipient retains them for collection for a period of six months or gives 30 days' notice of such availability before the end of the six-month period. Thereafter, the goods become an unconditional gift to the recipient. Goods are unsolicited if they are sent out without any prior request from the recipient.

Limited editions

Question: It greatly enhances the desirability of a product if it is called a 'limited edition'. What controls are there on the use of this technique?

Answer: The British Code of Advertising Practice allows editions to be limited by the number produced provided the promotion material clearly states the maximum number to be produced and the terms of the offer are in all respects clearly stated. The Code gives only grudging approval to editions limited by time, ie by the number of persons applying within a stated period of time. In such cases the word 'limited' or any of its derivatives may not be used without qualification and the advertiser must advertise his willingness to inform all interested purchasers of the number of articles eventually produced worldwide.

A statement in promotional literature that applications should be received by a certain date is not of itself the offer of a limited edition but difficulties have been experienced in the interpretation of the Code in this respect.

Identity of the promoter

Question: What are the rules about revealing the identity of promoters in promotional literature? Could we, for example, show only the name of our handling agents omitting any reference to ourselves?

Answer: Concealment of the true identity of a promoter would be contrary to the Code which requires that full information shall be given in relation to all promotions and that promotions shall be fair and honourable. The Advertising Standards Authority has adjudicated against numerous promotions where the promoter's proper name and address have not been given.

So far as the law is concerned the contracting party would be that named in the promotional material. It therefore follows that any action brought by a consumer would be against the company whose name appeared in the promotional material.

Question: But what about the situation where we use a travel company. Can't we give their name?

Answer: There is nothing wrong in giving the name of, for example, a travel company for the purpose of dealing with detailed questions concerning flights and hotels and questions of that sort. But under the Code the promoter remains responsible for *all* aspects of the promotion and, whilst a company can delegate some aspects of the execution of the promotion, it cannot delegate its overall responsibility.

Question: Are there any additional requirements as to identity in respect of mail order goods?

Answer: Yes. The Mail Order Transactions (Information) Order 1976 requires that all advertisements offering goods for which payment must be made before the goods are dispatched must contain in legible characters the name of the person carrying on the business, and the address at which the business in the course of which such orders are to be fulfilled, is managed.

It is also worth mentioning that all direct mail letters are legally required to give the proper name of the company. This is by virtue of Section 349 of the Companies Act 1985.

The British Code of Advertising Practice requires that all mail order advertisements should state clearly in the body of the advertisement (ie in a place other than a coupon) the true name or business name, as appropriate, of the advertiser and the full address at which his business is managed and at which he can be contacted during normal business hours. The address should normally be that of the advertiser himself.

CHAPTER 3
PRIZE DRAWS

Lotteries legislation

Question: I have been told I cannot run a sales promotion scheme if it is a lottery. Why does this matter?

Answer: The law of lotteries goes back a long way and predates the development of the sales promotion industry. The current law on lotteries, contained in the 1976 Lotteries and Amusements Act, prohibits lotteries unless they come within the specifically permitted types of lottery set out in the Act – basically private, society and local authority lotteries and the National Lottery. Since sales promotion lotteries are not exempted, the general ban prevents their use in sales promotion.

Question: Why does the law impose detailed constraints on the use of lotteries?

Answer: Historically, lotteries were seen to be a way of exploiting the poor. In the case of *Reader's Digest v Williams* (1976) the Lord Chief Justice said the purpose of the law had been '. . . to prevent those poor people who only had a few pence with which to buy food for their children from losing their money . . .'.

Question: What is a lottery?

Answer: A lottery has never been defined in any statute so it has been left to case law over the years to define it for us. In the case of *Reader's Digest v Williams* (1976), the Lord Chief Justice said:

> 'There are really three things one must look for in deciding whether a lottery has been

established. First of all, the distribution of prizes; secondly, the fact that that was to be done by means of chance; and thirdly, that there must be some actual contribution made *by the participants* in return for their obtaining a chance to take part in the lottery.' (Emphasis added.)

In other words, any game of total chance in which there is an award of prizes and people pay, directly or indirectly, to participate is a lottery.

Contribution

Question: What about a game of chance linked to the purchase of a product?

Answer: As we saw, for there to be a lottery there must be some element of contribution of payment to participate. Over the years a body of case law has been built up to show that product purchases or payment for a service would amount to a contribution. One of the most recent cases was the Player's 'Spot Cash' decision in 1980 *(Imperial Tobacco Ltd v HM Attorney-General)* in which scratch cards were included in some packets of Player's No 6 cigarettes. The price of the packets of cigarettes with scratch cards included were the same price as the packets that did not contain them. In addition, a small number of cards was available in dispensers in tobacconists. The House of Lords held it was a lottery because people were paying for their chance. Their Lordships were not impressed that the price was the same whether the packet contained a card or did not. And they thought the number of dispenser cards were too insignificant to affect their decision. Their Lordships said that to avoid being a lottery the game had to be free. There were two definitions of free. Firstly, there was free of any extra charge, and secondly there was free of any charge at all. To avoid being a lottery it had to be free of any charge.

Question: Supposing nobody knew about the game until after they had purchased?

Answer: If nobody buys in the knowledge and expectation of getting a chance it is not a lottery. In the case of *Minty v Sylvester* (1915) involving a theatre, on the first night of performance somebody mounted the stage and at random threw gold sovereigns into the audience. This was repeated on the second and subsequent days. The court held that on the first day it happened there was no lottery, because people buying their theatre tickets did not do so in the knowledge and expectation that by so doing they would have the opportunity of obtaining one of the gold sovereigns thrown out at random. However, as it became well known that this was happening at the theatre, on subsequent days it was held that people buying their theatre tickets were paying for a chance in the random distribution of gold sovereigns. Hence there was a lottery.

The problem is that the inability to announce a game before people have the opportunity to spend money means that this principle has little use in practice in sales promotion which, after all, is designed to increase sales.

Question: What happens if purchases are being made but not by the actual participants?

Answer: This situation often arises in respect of trade promotions where, for example, salesmen are being encouraged to sell more of a product by means of a draw. It is not, however, the salesman personally who buys the stock but his employer. Is this element of payment sufficient to establish a lottery? Opinions among lawyers differ but the author's view is that it does not. If one goes back to the definition of a lottery expounded in the case of

Reader's Digest v Williams (1976), one sees that the Lord Chief Justice talks of '... some actual contribution made by the participants ...' The participants in a trade promotion will be the employees and they are not themselves making any contribution. Accordingly, I believe that such schemes are not lotteries and are consequently lawful. One should, however, consider the points made about trade promotions in the chapter on bribery and corruption.

Question: If I give some of the proceeds to charity, doesn't this make the scheme legal?

Answer: No. Section 6 of the Lotteries and Amusements Act provides for what are termed 'Society Lotteries', ie lotteries promoted on behalf of a society which is established and conducted wholly or mainly for one of the following purposes:

(a) charitable purposes;

(b) participation in or support of athletic sports or games or cultural activities;

(c) purposes which are not described in (a) or (b) but are neither purposes of private gain nor purposes of any commercial undertaking.

However, the Act lays down stringent rules for such lotteries which include a limit on ticket prices, a requirement to get the scheme authorised by the society, the need to designate a member of the society as promoter, and the obligation to give all the resulting proceeds, after deduction of legitimate expenses, to the society.

Newspaper bingo and 'instant win'

Question: If you can't require people to spend money to partipate how do the newspaper bingo schemes fare?

Answer: The newspaper bingo schemes and the scratch card promotions run by some retailers and by major oil companies do not require purchases before participation. In the case of newspapers, one can borrow a paper from a friend, look at one in a public library, or usually ring up for the day's 'lottery' numbers from the paper concerned. It may be more convenient to buy the newspaper but it is open to anyone to participate without having to buy. The legal status of newspaper bingo schemes was confirmed in the case of *Express Newspapers v Liverpool Daily Post* (1985).

The garage promotions run on the same principle. One can drive in and just ask for a scratch card. The fact that very few people have the nerve to do this is irrelevant.

Question: Is it alright to invite those who do not want to buy the product to send in their name and address on a blank piece of paper? Does this legitimise the promotion?

Answer: Provided people can genuinely participate without product purchase, the answer would seem to be yes. However, the alternative route of participation should be made clear and purchasers and non-purchasers must be treated on equal terms. In correspondence with the Crown Prosecution Service, the CPS have advised me that in judging a free entry route, they expect that route to be 'genuine, realistic and unlimited'.

Question: What about 'Instant Win'?

Answer: Instant win mechanics have developed along with

plain paper entry schemes. They involve a consumer being able to tell whether they have won from the product purchased, without the necessity to take any further action. A non-purchase route is necessary to prevent such schemes constituting illegal lotteries.

Question: Does the method of selecting winners through the non-purchase route have to equate to the method that operates on-pack?

Answer: Some promoters have taken the view that the method by which winners are chosen from the free route must mirror the purchase route. Accordingly, they believe that if purchasers find out whether they are winners by opening a can, then cans must be opened on behalf of non-purchasers. Without it, they argue, you could be said to have two separate schemes.

Personally, I do not agree with this view. In a sense the two schemes are indeed separate, because one involves purchase and one involves sending off a plain paper entry. What unites them both is that they are part and parcel of the same promotion, with a common promotional budget and common prize fund.

One of the major objections to opening cans or packets of a product is that, as a proposition, it lacks credibility. That is not to say that promoters do not open cans when they say they will. But consumers find the whole notion unbelievable because they do not appreciate the reasons why promoters are doing it. And to present the consumer with an unbelievable proposition is to risk damaging the overall reputation of the promotion.

There is no reason why the selection should not be kept as similar to the on-pack operation as possible, whilst retaining credibility and cost-effectiveness. Instead of opening cans, a quantity of lids could be available from which a random selection can be made with broadly equivalent chances of success to those purchasing the product. But if necessary, I see nothing wrong with a straightforward computer selection system.

Question: Can I make participation in a game of chance dependent on participants doing something?

Answer: Yes, provided that what they do cannot be regarded as significant enough to amount to payment or contribution. For example, if a man was required to do an hour's work, or so, for which he would normally expect payment, this would probably be regarded as contribution. However, it is generally agreed that filling in questionnaires where a draw is an incentive to do so would be alright. So, too, would be inviting people to take, for example, a no-obligation test drive of a new car or to visit a showroom.

Telephone calls and postage

Question: Is there payment if people have to buy stamps or make phone calls to respond?

Answer: Although there are no known cases of successful prosecutions on this point, we do know that any payment does not necessarily have to be paid to the promoter for it to amount to contribution. On this basis, it is hard to see why an obligation to buy stamps or make phone calls should not, technically, be regarded as contribution. However, professional opinion is divided on this point, and some lawyers believe that the ordinary cost of 'phone calls or stamps can be regarded as 'incidental expenditure'.

More to the point, in a practical sense, is that games of chance now habitually ask for stamped envelopes for the free entry route. The authorities show no interest in pursuing the point, and the author's own correspondence with the Crown Prosecution Service suggests that they would not regard a test case as being in the public interest.

Question: If a lottery is a scheme based on chance, why can't I inject a little element of skill to take it outside the law. Surely it won't then be a lottery?

Answer: Yes and no. Yes, it is correct that an element of skill will stop the scheme being a lottery. No, this will not let you off the hook unless the nature of the game is changed to one in which skill is the deciding factor in the award of prizes, and not chance. This is because case law, particularly in the Player's Spot Cash case has shown that any element of skill will make a scheme a competition. In the next chapter we consider the law on competitions.

Prosecutions

Question: Who can be prosecuted for an illegal lottery?

Answer: Under the Lotteries and Amusements Act 1976, a number of people concerned with the arrangements for, and running of, an illegal promotion can be prosecuted. These include people who publish or distribute advertisements and people who use any premises for purposes connected with promoting or conducting an illegal lottery. Officers of a company can be prosecuted as well as the company itself, if the offence is due to their neglect, consent or connivance.

Question: What about foreign lotteries?

Answer: Section 2 of the 1976 Act makes it an offence in connection with any lottery promoted, or proposed to be promoted, either in Great Britain *or elsewhere,* to do certain things. These include printing, publishing or distributing any advertising of the lottery. It is therefore illegal to promote or be concerned in a foreign lottery to the same extent that it would be unlawful in relation to an English lottery. This restriction has been upheld by the European Court of Justice when section 2 was challenged under Community free movement rules.

Question: What about the rules for a free prize draw?

Answer: Promoters and their agencies should look at the list of items set out in clause 40 of the Sales Promotion Code, under the heading 'Promotions with prizes', and use the listings as appropriate. This is also discussed in the next chapter in the context of competitions.

Prizes

Question: Can I offer discounts as prizes?

Answer: Yes, in principle, provided that the discount is genuine and the original price was not inflated to make the discount possible. There is no problem in requiring people to pay in order to avail themselves of their prize so long as they did not have to pay to participate in the first place.

Chapter 4
COMPETITIONS

Definition

Question: What is a competition?

Answer: Like the term 'lottery', the term 'competition' is not statutorily defined. Again, as we noted in the last chapter, we have to look at case law. In the 1980 Spot Cash case, their Lordships said a competition was any game in which there was an element of skill – however small. For example, in *Hall v Cox* (1899), a scheme which involved predicting the number of births and deaths in a particular week was held to be a competition. However, in *Andrew v Stubbings* (1924), it was held that looking out for matches which lit with a green flame was not skill, but simple observation. It was not, therefore, a competition.

Illegal competitions

Question: When is a competition illegal?

Answer: Section 14 of the Lotteries and Amusements Act makes it unlawful to conduct, in or through any newspaper, or in connection with any trade or business of the sale of any article to the public:

(a) any competition in which prizes are offered for forecasts of the result either – (i) of a future event; or (ii) of a past event, the result of which is not yet ascertained, or not yet generally known;

(b) any other competition in which success does not depend to a substantial degree on the exercise of skill.

Section 14 of the Lotteries and Amusements Act therefore eliminates a whole range of types of competition. What they all have in common is that success cannot be said to be dependent on skill to any significant degree. In all the various types, chance is by far the overriding and dominant factor in success and the award of prizes.

Question: Could it not be said that the meeting of a panel of judges to decide on the winners of a competition is a future event and therefore covered by the prohibition on forecasting competitions in Section 14?

Answer: No. Such an interpretation would make most competitions illegal. In the case of *News of the World Ltd v Friend* (1973), one of the Law Lords said:

'. . . I cannot understand how it can be said that when in response to an invitation to take part in a competition a man sends in his answer to the problem posed he is, by sending in his answer, making a forecast of the result of the deliberations of the judges.'

Question: What then is meant by the term 'event'?

Answer: One has to distinguish between an event and what one might term a state of affairs. For example, the temperature on the roof of the London Weather Centre on a specified future date is not an event but a state of affairs. So, too, is an estimate of the state of the stock market on a future date. On the other hand, the outcome of a football match or a general election is clearly an event. Common sense is probably the best guide to what constitutes an event.

Having said that, one should not become overly concerned with what constitutes an event because a competition can still be caught by section 14(1)(c). This prohibits, as we saw above, any other competition in which success does not depend to a substantial degree on the exercise of skill.

Question: Can I require people to pay in some way in order to participate in a competition?

Answer: Yes, but it must be clear what the commitment is. If extra proofs of purchase are required this must be stated prominently and be available to potential participants before purchase. And if there is a requirement to provide a till receipt, as a proof of purchase, this must be stated before purchase as well.

Multi-stage schemes

Question: Must I always have a tie-breaker?

Answer: There is no automatic need to have two stages to a competition. Sometimes the 'tie-breaker' can be the one and only stage. However, if you are to have a first stage then you may need a way to select winners from the relatively large number of people who may have got the answers right to the first stage.

Question: Why can't I just put the entries with the right answer to the first stage into a hat and pull out winners that way?

Answer: In this situation, it would seem that the courts would regard each stage as separate and self-contained. This is particularly so when completing the first stage is a mere formality for the majority of contestants, and the second stage is the effective stage in determining winners and losers. If the second stage was pure chance and people had paid as a precondition for participation, the scheme would be a lottery and consequently illegal.

Question: How much skill do I need in a competition?

Answer: It is not a question of how much skill. Rather, it is a case of ensuring that skill is the deciding factor in the award of prizes. It is the degree to which success depends on skill rather than the degree of skill as such.

Particular types of competition

Question: What about 'spot the ball' competitions?

Answer: The legal status of 'spot the ball' competitions has never been satisfactorily and definitively settled. The problem is that whilst skill would probably get you to the general area in which the ball is located, where precisely the ball is must be a matter of pure chance. However, in the News of the *World Ltd v Friend* (1973) decision it was held that a 'spot the ball' competition did not fall foul of the ban on forecasting in section 14 because, as we saw earlier, the meeting of a panel of judges to decide where the ball was most likely to be was not an 'event' in itself.

In view of the wide preponderance of 'spot the ball' type schemes and the absence of any clear challenge on the point of legality it is probably safe, in practice, to run such schemes.

Question: Do ranking competitions present any special problems?

Answer: Ranking or factoral competitions, as they are sometimes known, are a popular form of competition but there are problems for both consumers and promoters alike. They involve putting a list of factors in order of importance.

Depending on the number of factors, it can be

virtually impossible to win a ranking competition because of the enormous number of possible variants. Some unscrupulous competition organisers have, therefore, organised ranking competitions knowing the chances of winning are infinitesimally small. They then offer a substantial case prize, say £1 million, and cover the very slight risk of winning by means of an insurance policy.

To deal with this problem, the Committee of Advertising Practice has advised that, if some advertised prizes may not be won, this fact should be made clear, and if the winning of a prize is distinctly unlikely that fact should be given special prominence.

It is advisable for a promoter to give a small pen picture of the sort of person whose judgement would be relevant to the list of factors. So, instead of saying 'just list these factors in order of importance', one should be more specific: 'List these factors in order of importance from the point of view of the modern busy housewife.' This makes the competition more focused and less open to the charge that it is simple guesswork.

Contractual issues

Question: The Lotteries and Amusements Act gives rise to criminal prosecution. Are there no civil law implications in respect of competitions?

Answer: Yes. When people enter a competition there is a contract between the participant and the promoter. This is one reason why it is so important to spend time on drafting the rules of the competition. Even free entry competitions can create a contractual relationship if some 'consideration' is involved. Breach of contract could be occasioned by a failure to run the competition properly, for example, by failing to follow the published methodology for selecting winners. For instance, in the case of *Chaplin v Hicks* (1911) a woman was awarded damages for the loss of a chance to win a beauty contest. She had lost that chance because of a breach of contract by the organisers. Another area of civil law that may be relevant is product liability. If a product supplied as a prize is defective and causes injury then a civil action will lie.

Competition rules

Question: Now I have established the basic legality of my promotion, what's next?

Answer: You must then make sure that the scheme meets all the requirements of the British Code of Sales Promotion Practice (the Code).

Question: What about the rules?

Answer: Clause 40 of the Code gives guidance on the construction of rules for competitions and other promotions with prizes. Getting the rules right is critically important for the interests of the promoter, as well as the consumer. Many subsequent arguments could have been avoided if more attention had been given to getting the rules set out clearly, comprehensively and unambiguously. The issues that should be covered by the rules are as follows:

1 the closing date;

2 any restriction on the number of entries or prizes which may be won;

3 any requirements for proof of purchase;

4 description of prizes;

5 any age, or other personal restrictions or any geographical restrictions;

6 how and when winners will be notified and results published;

7 the criteria for judging entries;

8 where appropriate, the ownership of copyright in entries;

9 if entries are returnable by the promoter, how they are to be returned;

10 how participants may obtain any supplementary rules which may apply – although these should not be rules which would reasonably affect the decision to purchase in the first place;

11 whether a cash alternative to any prize is available;

12 any permissions required, eg from parent or employer;

13 any intention to use winners in post-event publicity.

Question: Can I short-circuit the process?

Answer: Sometimes, it may not be possible to include all the necessary rules and competitors may have to be directed towards an address from which they can get the full rules. If this is done, the rules given 'up-front' must be those which have a direct bearing on whether the consumer decides to purchase and participate in the promotion. The Code says the items which should be made clear before purchase are:

(a) the closing date for receipt of entries;

(b) any geographical or personal restrictions such as location or age;

(c) any requirements for proofs of purchase;

(d) the need to obtain permission to enter from parents, employers or others;

(e) the nature of the prize(s).

Changing the goal posts

Question: What happens if I realise that I have misjudged things after the promotion has started?

Answer: Usually there is little that can be done. Sometimes the competition does not generate enough interest, for any number of reasons. Even so, the competition must be completed and prizes awarded – even if all the entrants qualify for prizes. Slippage of dates may be excusable if there is some good reason for it. Although it will rarely, if ever, be acceptable to delay the actual closing date, the date by which winners will be notified may slip because of unforeseeable circumstances. However, unless there is a very good reason indeed, such slippages could bring an infringement of the Code. In addition, it is worth remembering, as we have already noted, that when competitors take part in a promotional competition, there is a legally binding contract between the participants and the promoter. The rules are part of the contract and failure to abide by them is, on the face of it, a breach of contract.

Publicity

Question: How can I try and ensure that I get a publicity return from my promotion:

Answer: Two rules are particularly relevant here:

1 It is important to state whether or not there is a cash alternative to the prize. Failure to make it clear that there is no cash alternative to a prize has led some competitors, in the past, to refuse to attend a ceremony for the award of a prize.

2 The rules should, if appropriate, state that winners may be required to take part in publicity activities.

Chapter 5

INTELLECTUAL PROPERTY

Definitions

Question: What is intellectual property?

Answer: Intellectual property is the name we give to the branch of law that covers copyright, trade marks and patents.

Question: What do we mean by copyright?

Answer: Copyright is essentially a right in the creator of original material to control the reproduction of that material for as long as the material stays within copyright. Copyright exists basically in every original piece of literary, artistic, dramatic or musical work, and in sound recordings, films, television broadcasts, cable programmes and published editions.

Question: What is not subject to copyright protection?

Answer: The main exception to copyright protection is in respect of ideas and concepts. Although the tangible expression of an idea will be copyright, the idea itself is not copyright – although it may be protected in other ways, as we shall see later.

Another important exclusion from copyright protection relates to names, titles and slogans. In a well-known case earlier this century, no copyright was held to subsist in the slogan 'A youthful appearance is a social necessity, not a luxury'. However, it is interesting to note that copyright does exist in such items as train timetables and football fixture lists, not so much on the basis of the originality of the information, but on the basis of the work involved in gathering and presenting the material. Such documents are held to be compilations, and the legislation specifically provides that they are subject to copyright protection as literary works.

Ownership of copyright

Question: Who owns the copyright, and for how long?

Answer: The copyright belongs to the author of the copyright work, with the one exception that in the case of work created by employees in the course of their employment, the copyright belongs to their employer unless otherwise agreed. So, with work created in-house by employees of an advertising agency or sales promotion consultancy, the copyright would belong to the agency – but not work created by freelancers. The author of a work is normally the person who created it, though the rules are different for films and sound recordings.

Copyright in literary, artistic, dramatic or musical works currently lasts for life of the author plus 50 years, but a directive has been agreed at a European Union level which will soon bring about an extension of that period to life of the author plus 70 years.

Question: How do you copyright something?

Answer: It is a widely held belief that one can go through some process of registration, and thereby 'copyright' a piece of work. In the United Kingdom, as in most other countries, there is no process of registration that needs to be gone through because copyright protection arises automatically once a piece of work has been created to which copyright protection applies.

Ideas and concepts

Question: The most valuable part of a promotion is often the idea or concept. Are you really saying that this cannot be protected?

Answer: As we have already seen, there is no copyright in an idea or concept, so copyright protection cannot be used to protect a creative idea. However, that does not mean the idea is not capable of some protection by using other legal devices. The main way this can be done is by invoking what is known as the law of confidentiality. The law requires the following aspects to be present:

(a) that the circumstances in which the information was communicated import an obligation of confidence, in particular by making it clear to the other party that the material is copyright;

(b) the content of the idea is clearly identifiable, original, of potential commercial attractiveness and capable of reaching fruition.

This was well illustrated by what has become known as the 'Rock Follies' case (*Fraser and Others v Thames Television and Others* (1983)). Three members of the Rock Bottom pop group went to Thames Television and outlined their ideas for a new television series. They did so in circumstances which made it clear that the ideas were being communicated in confidence and this was also tied up in a contract by which Thames paid £500 for an option. Thames Television at that stage said they were not interested in the idea, but three years later a series was run by Thames Television based on the idea which had been presented to them.

Since the ideas and concepts had been presented in circumstances which imposed a duty of confidentiality on Thames Television, the suit against Thames Television was successful and the three individuals were awarded damages of £500,000.

Question: What if the idea is commonplace?

Answer: There is an old saying 'You can't make a silk purse out of a sow's ear'. In this context it means you cannot make a promotional idea or concept confidential if it is very much public property. So the idea of an instant win promotion could not be made confidential, unless the proposed use was highly innovative or presented in a very original way.

Moral rights

Question: I have heard about moral rights – what are they?

Answer: Moral rights are rights which belong to the author of a copyright literary, dramatic, musical or artistic work and to the director of a copyright film. Under the Copyright, Designs and Patents Act 1988, such rights cannot be assigned to anyone else, because they are personal rights. They can, however, be waived. So what are those moral rights?

1 *The right to be identified as author or director.* The right does not apply unless it has been asserted, either generally or specifically in relation to a particular use of the material. Such an assertion must be in writing, signed by the author or director or contained in a document which assigns the copyright.

There are a number of exceptions to the right, the most important of which, for agencies, is where use is made of copyright material by the copyright owner or with his consent, and where the copyright belongs to the author's or director's employer. In an agency situation, this would mean no moral rights would apply to employees and their work, provided that any usage was by the agency or with the agency's consent. Again, this would not include freelancers, and in their case, agencies need to think about waivers of moral rights.

2   *The right to object to derogatory treatment of work.* The law provides that an author or film director has the right not to have his work subjected to derogatory treatment.

What does this mean?

(a)   'Treatment' means any addition to, deletion from or alteration to, or adaptation of the work, other than a translation of a literary or dramatic work, or an arrangement or transcription of a musical work involving no more than a change of key or register.

(b)   'Derogatory' means any treatment which amounts to distortion or mutilation of the work, or is otherwise prejudicial to the honour or reputation of the author or director.

The right to object to derogatory treatment of work will not apply to employees unless they were identified at the time of the derogatory treatment, or were previously identified in or on published copies of the work.

Practical issues

Question: What must I consider in relation to copyright?

Answer: First, you must remember that most creative material will be copyright and, except for material created in-house in the course of employment, it will be necessary to make sure that the necessary assignments or usage licences are obtained. Also, you must remember to secure waivers of moral rights in respect of externally commissioned creative work.

Secondly, you need to protect your own creative material. As I have said, material is either subject to copyright protection or it is not. However, there are certain steps that one can take to reinforce one's claim to ownership of the copyright. It is important to keep copies of original drawings and other original creative material, in order to be ready for any challenge on ownership. It is also advisable to consider putting a 'C' in a circle and the word 'Copyright' against it, and perhaps the name of the copyright owner and the date; this should be used as a way of indicating that a particular piece of material is copyright and to act as something of a warning that the copyright owner will be likely to protect their interests.

Trade marks

Question: Where do trade marks fit in?

Answer: Under the Trade Marks Act 1994, registration is now possible for 'any sign capable of being represented graphically which is capable of distinguishing goods or services of one undertaking from those of other undertakings'.

The possibilities for registration under the new Act are now much greater. Under the Act, the following are now registerable for the first time: sounds, shapes, slogans and smells.

Slogans will only be registered where they can be shown to be distinctive. Most slogans are not distinctive and never will be because they are, to coin a phrase, 'here today – gone tomorrow'. And one should remember that it is no use going through the time and expense of an application for trade mark registration if the likelihood is that a new slogan will be in use by the time the procedural formalities have been completed.

Prior to the 1994 Act, any unauthorised use of a registered trade mark of another company in Part A of the register would have been an infringement. However, the law has been changed, ostensibly to facilitate genuine comparative advertising. Whether the change will have this effect remains to be seen.

Question: When can trade marks be used?

Answer:
1. The most obvious circumstance in which a registered trade mark can be used is where there is permission or authority to use the mark. Sometimes that will be express permission, although there are many circumstances in which there is implied consent. For example, if the purpose of a promotion is to promote the sales of the goods which have the mark on them, then it is reasonable to assume that there is implied permission for that exposure and use of the mark because it is necessary to assist in the marketing of the relevant goods.

2. As we have seen already, a trade mark can be used to identify the goods or services of another, but it must be in accordance with honest industrial or commercial practices. If not, the use will be treated as infringing the trade mark if the use takes unfair advantage of, or is detrimental to, the distinctive character or repute of the mark.

Question: How can I check out trade marks?

Answer: If there is any doubt about whether a mark is

registered, then the easiest course is to apply for a search through a trade mark agent. This is a relatively inexpensive process, and will enable a report to be made which will reveal what is registered and in respect of what classes of goods. The existence of an 'R' in a circle will indicate a registered mark – to use such a device when a mark is not registered is a criminal offence.

Question: What are the consequences of an infringement of copyright or registered trade mark?

Answer: Damages are possible as compensation for an infringement of copyright or a registered trade mark although, if the damage suffered is relatively slight in commercial terms, it is unlikely that the amount of damages that a court would award would make it worthwhile pursuing a case to full trial. In most cases, the only remedy worth having for an infringement of copyright or a registered trade mark is an injunction, which puts an end to the relevant infringement. An application for an injunction can be made before a full trial but, if the application for an injunction is unsuccessful, in most cases the matter does not proceed to a full hearing.

Patents

Question: What are patents?

Answer: Patents were first granted in the reign of Elizabeth I to facilitate the growth of new industries. Patents encourage industrial innovation by giving the inventor of an industrial technique a monopoly right to exploit that invention for a period of 20 years – after which the invention is considered to be in the public domain.

However, patent protection does not protect innovative design, but only the essential function.

Question: When do patents become relevant to sales promotion?

Answer:
1 In relation to the production of promotional merchandise, it is important to make sure that no existing patents are infringed. This is particularly important given the widespread importation of promotional merchandise from countries in the Far East such as China and Korea.

2 Occasionally, in developing a new promotional technique, or developing a novel way of presenting an existing promotional technique, a device is produced which is patentable. One example that has come my way over the years related to a drinks can with a device that enabled money to pop out when winning cans were opened. This was an invention, and an application was made to patent this device. This does not happen very often, but sales promotion practitioners should be aware of the possibility.

Chapter 6
PRICE PROMOTIONS

The law relating to price promotions is now mainly contained in Part III of the Consumer Protection Act 1987.

Section 20 of the Consumer Protection Act 1987 prohibits the giving by any means in the course of a business an indication which is misleading as to the price at which any goods, services, accommodation or facilities are available. This new offence is very widely based as the following examples will reveal.

Guidance as to what is or is not misleading is given in a Code of Practice for Traders on Price Indications issued by the Department of Trade and Industry (The Code) (see Appendix 2 below). This Code enjoys a unique status in law. Its recommendations are not mandatory, by which we mean that a price indication not covered by the Code would not of itself be misleading and therefore unlawful. However, compliance with the Code would constitute a defence of 'all due diligence and all reasonable precautions' as provided by section 39(1) of the Act. Furthermore, a court may have regard to the recommendations in the Code in determining whether or not a particular price indication is unlawful.

Indications that a price is less than it actually is

Question: We have often heard of self-service retailers being prosecuted for selling goods at a higher price than indicated. Is that still an offence and can it affect goods subject to promotions?

Answer: The offence of charging a higher price at the checkout than appears on the goods or on a shelf-edge marker is one of the oldest pricing problems for retailers. It is known in the trade as 'buncing'. It was first prohibited by the Trade Descriptions Act 1968, since when many retailers have fallen foul of it. Rarely is it done deliberately; most often it is simply carelessness in failing to alter marked prices or bar codes on old stock when prices are increased.

Section 21 of the Consumer Protection Act 1987, which gives meaning to the term 'misleading' in section 20, states that a price is misleading if it indicates that the price is less than it in fact is. Indeed, the law is even wider in its application than the old Act for it stipulates that a price indication can become misleading after it is given; the offence is committed if some or all consumers might reasonably be expected to rely on the price indication after it is given and; the person who gives the indication fails to take all such steps as are reasonable to prevent consumers from relying on the indication.

The indicated price for goods which are offered with incentives can all too easily be caught by this offence.

Question: How can incentive goods be caught by the suggestion that the price is less than it actually is?

Answer: It is most likely to arise where prices have changed immediately before or after a promotion with stock of the promoted goods remaining on display simultaneously with standard non-promoted packs. It is basically a question of controlled stock rotation.

Reductions from a previous price

Question: How can genuine reductions in prices be indicated?

This is the most straightforward of all price comparisons provided it complies with the following basic rules:

(a) the higher and the reduced price must be shown;

(b) the higher price must be the last price at which the goods were offered in the previous six months;

(c) the product should have been available to consumers at the higher price for at least 28 days in the preceding 6 months*;

(d) the previous price should have been offered for that period at the same shop where the reduced price is now being offered.

*The 28-day rule does not apply to food and drink or non-food perishables if they have a shelf life of less than 6 weeks.

For full guidance as to reduced prices see paragraph 1.2 of the Code (Appendix 2, below).

Question: If it is impossible to satisfy these rules can a disclaimer be used?

Answer: No. The old disclaimers such as 'higher prices have not necessarily been on offer for a continuous period of 28 days in the preceding 6 months' were specifically provided for in the Trade Descriptions Act 1968. The present law makes no such provision. To avoid committing the new offence, positive statements rather than disclaimers are required in order that price comparisons are fair and reasonable.

Question: What positive statement would suffice if the 28-day rule had not been complied with?

Answer: The actual period during which the higher price had been on offer should be stated, eg 'SALE — £25 Previous price £30 offered from 1 to 15 December'.*

Question: What positive statement would suffice if the goods had not been previously offered at the higher price in the same shop?

Answer: An indication of the shops where they had been offered is required, eg 'These goods were on sale at the higher price in our five largest stores'.*

*These examples of positive statements would not be acceptable in all cases. If, to take an extreme case, a higher price had only been on offer for a very short period indeed, say one hour, the price indication may be misleading even though a positive statement had been made. The same might be the case if a very large multiple company with 300 stores had offered the goods at the higher price in only one or two of those stores. In all cases the comparison must be fair and reasonable notwithstanding the use of positive statements.

Question: How do these rules apply to catalogue or mail order traders?

Answer: Any comparison with a previous price should be with the price in the trader's own last issued catalogue, advertisement or leaflet. If the product is offered in both catalogues etc and shops the higher price should be the last price at which the goods were offered. In all other respects the rules given above apply.

Question: Can we offer a series of reductions on the same goods?

Answer: Yes. The Code makes allowance for circumstances where it is wished to make further reductions during the same sale or special offer period. Only the highest price need comply with the 28-day rule. See paragraph 1.2.6 of the Code (Appendix 2, below).

Question: Are there any restrictions as to how a genuine previous price must be indicated?

Answer: The expressions used must be clear. Thus 'normal price', 'regular price' or 'usual price' should not be used alone. They should be qualified to show that they are the seller's own previous price, eg 'our normal price'.

Recommended prices

Question: Can we compare our selling prices with genuine manufacturers' recommended prices?

Answer: Yes, provided you comply with the following rules:

(a) initials or abbreviations may not be used except for 'RRP' to describe a recommended retail price and 'man rec price' to indicate a manufacturer's recommended price. In all other cases the basis of the comparison with a recommended price must be spelt out in full;

(b) the recommended price must have been recommended to the retailer by the manufacturer or supplier as a price at which the product might be sold to consumers;

(c) the retailer must deal with the manufacturer or supplier on normal commercial terms; and

(d) the recommended price is not significantly higher than prices at which the product is generally sold at the time the comparison is first made.

Question: How can we judge whether a recommended price is not significantly higher than prices at which the product is generally sold?

Answer: Common sense is the best guide to what is a reasonable recommended price, particularly when supported by a survey of prices charged for comparable goods.

It is the retailer's responsibility to consider whether a recommended price is consistent with prices generally being offered for the goods concerned but it should be pointed out that the offence in section 20 of the Act can be committed by any company giving misleading indications of price to consumers. As yet there are no judicial precedents on this point but it is entirely possible that a manufacturer who recommends a price which is commercially unrealistic may commit an offence.

Question: What is the difference between a recommended price and resale price maintenance?

Answer: Resale price maintenance occurs when a manufacturer or supplier seeks to compel retailers to sell goods supplied to them at a minimum price. The Resale Prices Act 1976 makes such practices unlawful. Whenever a manufacturer or supplier wishes to recommend retail selling prices he must make it clear that it is merely a recommendation and not a minimum price.

Question: It is often the case that manufacturers print a selling price on packs. How can a retailer sell below that price if he does not wish to obliterate it from the pack?

Answer: The Code recognises this problem and provides that such printed prices may be regarded as recommended prices by the retailer without the need to indicate that they are recommended prices. The retailer is therefore free to offer the goods at a lower price and to mark that lower price on the packs without first obliterating the manufacturer's marked price. This does not apply to retailers' own-label packs.

Question: What is a retailer's responsibility where the manufacturer marks goods with flash offers, eg '10p off RRP'?

Answer: The offer must be honoured by the retailer unless he chooses to obliterate it. Redeemable coupons or vouchers are not subject to these requirements (see Chapter 10). For Code requirements as to recommended prices see paragraphs 1.6 and 1.7 thereof (Appendix 2, below).

Introductory offers

Question: Introductory offers are important for the launching of new products or businesses. What are the rules?

Answer: A promotion must not be called an introductory offer unless it is the intention to continue to offer the product for sale after the offer period is over and at a higher price. The offer must have a reasonably imminent end or it could become misleading to call it an introductory offer. The period may vary depending on the nature of the product and its shelf life. Under the old legislation there was a specific requirement to give the expiry date of the offer. That has not been repeated but it is very unlikely that such an offer could be deemed to be misleading if an expiry date is given and the price which will pertain after that date is quoted. However, the Code suggests that an after-promotion price should only be given if the trader is certain that, subject only to circumstances beyond his control, identical products will continue to be offered at the higher price for at least 28 days in the three months after the end of the offer period or after the offer stocks run out. This suggestion has been criticised because the purpose of many introductory offers is to test public response to a new product and if demand is heavy it may be impossible to honour the 28-day period. It must be assumed, until a court rules otherwise, that heavy and unexpected demand would be deemed to be circumstances beyond control.

Question: If demand is lower than expected may an introductory offer be extended?

Answer: Yes. The Code requires a positive statement such as 'extended for a further two weeks until 1 June' to make it clear that the period has been extended.

For the suggestions as to introductory offers see paragraph 1.3 of the Code (Appendix 2, below).

Question: Can we avoid the rules on introductory offers by calling the offer an 'after-promotion price'?

Answer: No, the rules are the same for both types of promotion. It is also necessary to state in full what is meant whenever future prices are quoted, ie 'after-sale price' not 'ASP' and 'after-promotion price' not 'APP'.

Comparisons with other traders' prices

Question: Can comparisons be made with other traders' prices?

Answer: The government recognises that competition in the market is beneficial to consumers and it is therefore necessary to permit fair comparisons with other traders' prices. The Code, however, makes it difficult to do so without risking the commission of an offence. The rules are:

(a) the quoted 'other trader's price' must be accurate and up-to-date. This is nearly impossible to achieve because as soon as the other trader learns of the comparison he is likely to reduce his price thereby making the comparison misleading;

(b) the name of the other trader must be clearly and prominently stated with the price comparison;

(c) the shop where the other trader's price applies must be identified if he is in fact trading from a shop; and

(d) the other trader's price relates to the same products or substantially similar products. Any differences between the products must be stated clearly.

Question: Can general statements about prices charged by other traders be made?

Answer: The Code refers to price promise statements such as 'if you can buy this product elsewhere for less, we will refund the difference' and requires that such statements should not be made in relation to 'own-brand' products which other traders do not stock unless the offer will also apply to other traders' equivalent goods. Further, if there are any conditions attached to such offers they must be clearly stated.

Comparisons with other traders' prices are always difficult and, to some extent, dangerous. They are more likely to succeed in relation to mail order offers where the other traders' prices are quoted in a catalogue and cannot be easily changed.

Question: Are there any other problems with comparisons with other traders' prices?

Answer: If another trader's price is incorrectly stated not only would the trader making the comparison face the possibility of criminal proceedings under part III of the Consumer Protection Act 1987 but the offended trader may sue for damages for loss of business. It is a technique which should be used with the greatest care.

Basket of goods comparisons can create problems where one retailer compares a range of their goods with those of another retailer. In such cases, it is important to make sure that one is comparing like with like. It is also important to make it clear when the comparison was made. Prices change quickly and the comparison needs to be presented as a snapshot in time. A note of guidance on basket of goods comparisons can be obtained from the Advertising Standards Authority.

References to value or worth

Question: What about general statements concerning the value or worth of goods offered?

Answer: The Code prohibits comparisons of selling prices with amounts described only as 'worth' or 'value'. General advertising slogans and statements about general trading practice, such as 'low prices is our policy', or innocuous statements such as 'unbeatable value' or 'the greatest value in town' are considered to be advertisers' puffery and are not seen as price claims.

The test to be considered in each case is whether the slogan or words used are likely to suggest a comparison with another price in the minds of consumers. The law requires that all price comparisons be capable of substantiation.

Sales and special events

Question: In a 'sale' is it necessary that all goods offered should have been previously offered at a higher price?

Answer: There is nothing to prevent reduced goods being

sold side by side with other goods which have not been reduced or further goods which have been brought in specially for the sale provided that each group of goods is clearly identified. Goods which have been reduced should be marked with the original higher price; the reduced price; and be distinguished from other goods which have not been reduced. Merchandise being sold at its normal price should be separately displayed so that there can be no doubt that it is not a part of the sale. Goods brought in for the event should be marked 'special purchase' or something similar, and should not be double priced.

Question: Is it in order to use general price statements such as 'half-marked price'?

Answer: Yes, provided you also indicate the higher and lower prices on each item of merchandise and take care that all reductions are in fact at least 50%.

Question: What about statements such as 'up to 50% off'?

Answer: The Code requires that at least 10% of the range of products on offer should have been reduced by 50%. For 'Sales' and 'Special Events' see paragraph 1.9 of the Code (Appendix 2, below).

Price comparisons in different circumstances

Question: Is it still permitted to quote different prices for different quantities of goods?

Answer: Yes. You can offer, for example, '£1 each, 4 for £3.50'.

62 Price promotions

Question: What about different prices for goods in different condition?

Answer: It is acceptable to quote 'seconds £20, when perfect £30' etc. The 'when perfect' price should have been previously charged by the trader concerned and the 28-day rule and the rules as to different shops should be followed. If the 'when perfect' price is a recommended price then the rules on p 55 should be followed and if it is another trader's price then the rules on p 58 should be followed.

Question: Can different prices be charged depending on the availability of the goods?

Answer: It is in order to quote different prices such as 'Price £50 — when specially ordered £60'. The test is whether the different circumstances are clearly stated.

Question: What are the rules for different prices for goods in a different state?

Answer: This usually applies to goods available both in kit form and ready-assembled form. The rules are that it is in order to quote 'Price in kit-form £50, price ready-assembled £70' but the Code suggests that a third of the total stock should be in the different state, eg ⅓ ready assembled and ⅔ in kit form or vice versa in the same shop. If another trader's price for one or other of the different states is being used as a basis for comparison then the rules described on p 58, above should be followed.

Question: Is it still in order to quote different prices for different groups of people?

Answer: Yes, this is another principle which has not been changed. It is in order to quote, for example, 'senior citizens price £2.50 — others £5'. The Code, however, gives further advice by stating that words such as 'our normal price' or 'our regular price' should not be used to describe the higher price unless it applies to at least half of the trader's customers.

For Code requirements as to different circumstances see part 1.4 (Appendix 2, below).

Post and packing etc charges

Question: Must prices quoted to consumers always include postage, packing and other ancillary charges?

Answer: Yes. The Price Indications Code is quite specific about this and it applies to mail order traders and shops who offer a delivery service. See paragraph 2.2.4 and 2.2.5 of the Code (Appendix 2, below). The Price Marking Order 1991 requires prices to be all inclusive of non-optional ancillary charges, or for their cost to be clearly shown.

VAT

Question: Do the same rules apply to VAT inclusive prices?

Answer: Where transactions with consumers are concerned all quoted prices should be VAT inclusive. For business contracts see paragraph 2.2.7 of the Code (Appendix 2, below). If rates of VAT should change the correct VAT inclusive price should be communicated to consumers before they are committed to a purchase. As with ancillary charges, the 1991 Price Marking Order normally requires VAT-inclusive prices to be shown.

Mail order trade

Question: How long do prices in mail order catalogues remain current?

Answer: The Act and the Code are quite specific that prices which are correct at the time they are given can become misleading later and constitute an offence. This applies if consumers could reasonably be expected still to be relying on prices quoted in catalogues and the mail order trader had not taken all reasonable steps to prevent them from doing so.

Consequently, if prices stated in a current catalogue have to be changed, the very least which should be done is to ensure that anyone who orders goods at the old price is advised of the new price before being committed to the purchase. See paragraph 3.1 of the Code (Appendix 2, below).

Newspaper and magazine advertisements

Question: For how long are prices quoted in newspaper and magazine advertisements expected to remain current?

Answer: The Code suggests that the period should be a reasonable one and generally not less than seven days. Much would depend on the frequency of publication and whether any indication of possible changes in price was given in the advertisement. See paragraph 3.2 of the Code (Appendix 2, below).

Other price indications

Question: Is there any legislation which requires the selling price of goods to be stated?

Answer:	Yes. The Price Marking Order 1991 requires that the unit price must be indicated for goods sold from bulk, goods pre-packed in variable quantities and, from 7 June 1995, for certain goods pre-packed in pre-established quantities. Special provisions are included to deal with the unit pricing of cheese, meat and milk pre-packed in pre-established quantities, and the metric and imperial units of measurement to be used for the unit pricing of food and other goods are specified.
Question:	What is the position with prices when people pay with credit cards?
Answer:	A trader does not have to charge the same price to cash and credit card customers. However, if the price varies depending on the method of payment, the Price Indications (Method of Payment) Regulations 1991 requires that a clear explanatory statement be given.

Vouchers and coupons

Question:	What are the rules about offering vouchers or coupons as an alternative to price promotions?
Answer:	The offer of vouchers, coupons, container attachments etc is a useful alternative to direct reductions in price or comparisons with other prices. It is only in certain very unlikely circumstances that there could be a breach of criminal law in relation to a coupon etc promotion. For example, if a collection of a number of bottle tops were offered as a discount against the price of a further purchase of the product and that discount was not honoured it could be argued that there was an offence against section 20 of the Consumer Protection Act 1987 in that there was a misleading indication of the price to be paid for the further purchase. To the best of my knowledge, there has never been such a case

but it is possible that such an offence could be committed.

In all other respects the offer of coupons etc is free from statutory control under part III of the 1987 Act because it does not relate to an indication of price. However, regard must be had to the Sales Promotion Code which requires that the following should be easily seen and understood by consumers:

(a) the method of making use of the opportunity presented by the sales promotion, or of obtaining the goods, services, facilities or refunds on offer;

(b) the nature and number of any proofs of purchase required; and

(c) the cost and conditions of participation in the promotion including methods of payment and amounts of any additional postage or delivery charges.

Any instructions as to how a consumer may participate in a sales promotion should give the full name of the promoter and the address at which he can be contacted during normal business hours.

When such instructions require participants to detach and return a response coupon, the address of the promoter should appear in the material which can be retained by the participant.

There are notes for guidance on best practice in respect of coupons created by the Institute of Sales Promotion and endorsed by all the key organisations concerned with the creation and use of coupons. The notes for guidance are set out as Appendix 3.

CHAPTER 7

FREE AND EXTRA VALUE INCENTIVES

This chapter deals with the offer of free additional goods or services and extra value offers, such as additional quantity in the pack.

Free offers

Question: If goods or services are offered 'free' does this mean that they must be wholly free or can minor ancillary charges, such as postage and packing, be made?

Answer: The unqualified use of the word 'free' in a promotion means that there can be no charges of any kind. The Code requires that offers should not be described as free if there is any direct cost to the consumer, other than a charge not exceeding, as appropriate:

- current public rates of postage;

- the actual cost of freight or delivery of the promotional goods;

- the cost, including incidental expenses, of any travel involved if the consumer collects the offer.

In all cases, the consumer's liability for such costs should be made clear, and there should be no additional charges for packing or handling.

Complaints to the Advertising Standards Authority (ASA) about misleading offers of 'free' goods and services form one of the most frequent and persistent problems for the sales promotion business.

For full details of the Sales Promotion Code requirements as to free offers see clause 39 of the Code (Appendix 1).

Misleading statements about free offers may also be unlawful under section 20 of the Consumer Protection Act 1987. The Department of Trade and Industry Code of Practice for Traders on Price Indication (see Chapter 6) requires that consumers should be told exactly what they must buy to get the free offer. There are similar provisions to those above in the Sales Promotion Code: see part 1.10 of the DTI Code (Appendix 2, below).

Question: Is it necessary to be specific about the finish dates for free offers?

Answer: Yes. The date on which free offers conclude should always be stated clearly in advertising material.

Question: The offer of free goods sometimes involves fitting before the free goods can be used by consumers. How can misunderstandings about this be prevented?

Answer: By making it absolutely clear in the promotional material what is offered. A statement such as 'Special Offer Windows Fitted Free' leaves the consumer in doubt as to whether the whole deal, ie windows and fitting, are free, or whether it is intended to offer free fitting only. If words such as 'Windows purchased during our special offer period will be fitted free' had been used the problem would not arise.

Question: Sometimes goods are of a type which are rarely fitted by consumers themselves. Is it still necessary to make it clear that a free offer applies only where fitting is carried out?

Answer: Of course. The ASA has upheld complaints on this very point. In one case a buyer who responded to an advertisement stating 'Free Offer Gas Effect Fire or Equivalent Fire Side Items If You Buy A Design Fireplace Now' was refused the gas effect fire on the grounds that it only applied where the fireplace was fitted by the advertiser. The ASA upheld the complaint because the offer was not sufficiently specific. If the words 'fitted by us' had been added to the offer all would have been well. Such matters are now also caught by section 21(1)(b) of the Consumer Protection Act 1987.

Question: Are there any other problem areas in regard to free incentives?

Answer: One phenomenon has been the offer of free travel and accommodation in relation to time-share business; free wine with meals at selected restaurants; free allocations of petrol with new cars; and free audio and video cassettes by different performers. By their very nature, such promotions tend to be rather complex and require very careful drafting to ensure that each feature of the offer is easily understood by consumers. The offer of free travel and accommodation is now also subject to the Package Travel, Package Holidays and Package Tour Regulations 1992.

Question: Can the problems associated with free offers be overcome by calling them 'gifts'?

Answer: No. A gift is not a gift if it involves any payment and the rules explained above should be adhered to.

Question: Can a value be ascribed to free goods, such as 'A valuable set of wine glasses worth £40 free when you buy a case of Nuit St Georges'?

Answer: No. The DTI Code on Price Indications (paragraph 1.10.3) (see Appendix 2, below) requires that where any value is ascribed to a free offer it must be done as if the free offer were itself being sold. By this we mean that the trader would have to state his usual selling price for the free goods, a recommended price or another trader's price etc. Unsupportable references to 'worth' or 'value' would be unlawful.

Extra value packs

Question: What are the rules about adding additional quantities to a standard pack of a product, and flashing '10% extra'?

Answer: This is entirely in order provided that the additional quantity is included in the declaration of contents, if required. The additional quantity could also be indicated by a band around the top of the container which fairly represents 10% of the capacity of the standard pack.

Question: You refer to declarations of quantity above as being necessary 'if required'. Are such declarations not necessary on all packaged goods?

Answer: Regulations made under the Weights and Measures Act 1985 provide that certain classes of goods must be marked with a statement of quantity, either by weight, volume, capacity measurement, length or number, whilst others may be so marked if required. Yet other goods are wholly exempted from such declarations or are partially so when packed with other goods or in multiple packs. If goods are marked with a declaration of quantity either because they must be or because the packer wishes to do so, that declaration must be for the net contents of the pack including the additional quantity. The presence of the additional quantity could be declared separately in addition to the statutory declaration, eg '250g + 25g — now 275g'.

Question: Are there any additional considerations if we wish to claim that the extra quantity is free?

Answer: It is necessary to ensure that there has been no recent increase in the price of the standard pack immediately before or coincidental with the introduction of the extra quantity pack so that an allegation that the price has been increased to pay for the additional quantity cannot be made. The extra quantity pack must be offered by each retailer at the same price as the standard pack and ideally that price should have prevailed for at least 28 days before the introduction of the extra quantity pack.

Question: What are the problems about offering extra quantity in products subject to prescribed pack ranges?

Answer: Where a product is required to be made up in prescribed pack sizes there is a danger that a pack with a certain amount extra may not fall into the next highest prescribed pack size. For example, biscuits are required to be made up in quantities of 100g, 125g, 150g, 200g, 250g, 300g or a multiple of 100g up to 5 kg. Packs of 85g or less are exempted. If it was decided to offer 10% extra on a 250g pack, for example, the new pack would be 275g and that is not a permitted pack size. The pack would be unlawful. The only alternatives are to pack to the next prescribed size above the standard pack, ie 300g in the example given, thus offering 20% extra, or to offer a small pack of 25g banded to the standard pack thus keeping the extra quantity to the desired 10%.

Question: Which products are subject to prescribed pack sizes?

Answer: At the moment they are mainly foodstuffs, including these product categories: barley, rice and similar cereals, certain biscuits, bread, cereal breakfast foods, chocolate products, cocoa products, coffee and coffee mixtures, dried fruits, dried vegetables, edible fats, flour, honey, jams and similar products, jelly preserves, milk, molasses, syrup and treacle, oat products, pasta, potatoes, salt, sugar and tea. There are numerous exemptions and qualifications of these categories. Non-food products are limited at present to solid fuel. However, EC requirements will soon be implemented and a much wider range of foodstuffs and non-food products will be subject to prescribed pack sizes.

It is recommended that professional advice be sought on all extra quantity promotions for products subject to prescribed pack sizes.

Multiple packs

Question: Are there any problems with the 'get one extra free' or 'three for the price of two' etc type of promotion with packs banded together?

Answer: The advice above about recent price increases should be observed. In multiple packs the compulsory labelling requirements of regulations made under the Weights and Measures Act 1985 and/or the Food Act 1984 should be borne in mind. For food products it is necessary that the product name, the list of ingredients, the minimum durability date, the name and address of the packer or seller, the indication of origin and instructions for use or storage if required and the statement of quantity must be clearly visible. For non-foods the basic requirement is the statement of quantity but there are special additional labelling requirements in relation to cosmetics, medicinal products and certain dangerous products. If all of the information required by law can be seen through the banding all is well. If it cannot be seen then the information must be repeated on the banding or outer packaging. In most cases, it will be necessary to give an overall statement of quantity, eg '5 x 250g' in addition to the weight marking of '250g' on each individual pack.

Chapter 8

MAIL ORDER AND DIRECT MARKETING PROMOTIONS

Sales promotions for goods distributed by way of mail order or direct response are, of course, subject to all the rules applicable to promotions through retail shops. Identification of the mail order trader is important and regard should be had to the Mail Order Transactions (Information) Order 1976 (see Chapter 2, above). By virtue of the fact that the supplier and buyer do not meet face to face, there are a few additional considerations about sales promotion generally and points to be remembered about trading lists.

Some general rules about mailed promotions

Question: What are the additional controls on mail order and direct response promotions?

Answer: They are:

(a) Clause 52 of the British Code of Advertising Practice, which contains special provisions for what is termed 'distance selling'. In certain circumstances they will affect sales promotions (see below);

(b) the Direct Marketing Association (DMA) operates a Code of Practice which, in its general requirements, imposes standards of fair trading consistent with those of the Advertising and Sales Promotion Codes. It is directly binding only on members of DMA;

(c) the Data Protection Act 1984, which imposes special requirements as to mailing lists and their use. Clause 53 of the Advertising Code has rules on list and database practice, covering the use of personal data for advertising and direct marketing purposes.

Question: Are there any particular requirements about product standards and descriptions bearing in mind that consumers do not see the goods before purchase?

Answer: Where appropriate, goods supplied by mail order or direct response shall conform to relevant British Standards. This is particularly the case in regard to product safety (see Chapter 10, below). All such products should conform to any description given of them in an advertisement or catalogue and to any samples which may have been sent. It should always be remembered that the contract is made on the description of the goods given in the catalogue or advertisement. Any non-conformity with the description would be a breach of contract (see Chapter 2).

Note: that the above considerations apply equally to the substantive goods of the contract and incentive goods.

Question: Certain goods are not acceptable for sale by mail order etc. What are they?

Answer: Section 11 of the 1953 Post Office Act prohibits the sending of certain articles by post. These include any dangerous or noxious substances, or anything likely to injure postal staff. Also included are indecent or obscene paintings, prints, photographs or films.

Question: What are the restrictions on promotional products which may be addressed to children or which may attract them?

Answer: Clause 47.5 of the Advertising Code provides that promotions addressed to children:

(a) should not encourage excessive purchases in order to participate;

(b) should make clear that parental permission is required if prizes and incentives might cause conflict between children and their parents. Examples include animals, bicycles, tickets for outings, concerts and holidays;

(c) should clearly explain the number and type of any additional proofs of purchase needed to participate;

(d) should contain a prominent closing date;

(e) should not exaggerate the value of prizes or the chances of winning them.

Unsolicited promotional goods

Question: Can unsolicited promotional goods be sent to consumers?

Answer: There is nothing to prevent unsolicited goods being sent to consumers but it is an offence against the Unsolicited Goods and Services Act 1971, as amended, to demand payment for them or to make any threat as to payment. Further, if unsolicited goods are sent to a consumer he or she is entitled to treat them as an unconditional gift if the sender does not take possession of them within a six-month period from the day they were received, or not less than 30 days from the end of the six-month period the consumer gives notice to the sender and the sender does not take possession of them within 30 days of the receipt of the notice.

Unsolicited goods are any goods sent out without any prior request being made by the consumer.

Question:	Are there any products which may not be sent out unsolicited?
Answer:	It is an offence against section 4 of the Unsolicited Goods and Services Act 1971, as amended to send to any person any book, magazine or leaflet or any advertising material for any such publication, which he knows or ought reasonably to know is unsolicited and which describes or illustrates human sexual techniques.
Question:	Is it an offence for book or records clubs to send out further goods in error after a member has cancelled his or her subscription?
Answer:	In principle goods sent out by a club after cancellation of a subscription are unsolicited. However, before an offence can be proven the prosecution must show that the club did not have 'reasonable cause to believe' that there was a right to payment. In *Reader's Digest Association Ltd v Pirie* (1973) a member had cancelled his subscription but continued to receive books and demands for payment. The error arose because a junior employee had not altered the company's computer to show that the subscription had been cancelled. It was held on appeal that it could not be said that the company did not have reasonable cause to believe that there was a right to payment and the conviction in the lower court was quashed.
Question:	What about hoax orders or orders bearing an incorrect name or address?
Answer:	This is a problem for all mail order or direct response companies. However, in *Corfield v World Records Ltd* (1979) the Divisional Court considered an appeal by the prosecutor against the dismissal of a case by the lower court where an order had been received from a Mr M Colebune in response to which records had been sent out. At the address given lived a boy named M Colebourne but neither

he nor his parent had ordered the records. The court took the view that either Colebune and Colbourne were one and the same person in which case the goods were not unsolicited, or that they were two separate people, in which case the threats as to payment were not directed at M Colebourne. The appeal was dismissed.

Trading lists

Question: What are the likely consequences arising from errors in mailing lists?

Answer: Where mailing lists containing the names and addresses of individual consumers are kept on a computer, the requirements of the Data Protection Act 1984 apply. The Act requires that data shall be accurate and where necessary, kept up to date. Personal data is inaccurate if it is incorrect or misleading as to any matter of fact. The most common problems associated with mailing lists are: the name of deceased persons remaining on the lists, thereby causing distress to close relatives; persons included on the list moving to a different address but mailed advertising for them continuing to arrive at the old address; or name and addresses changing because of marriage or divorce. Where there is evidence of significant breach of this requirement the Data Protection Registrar could take administrative action by way of a cancellation of, or condition attached to, registration or he could, in extreme cases, prosecute. Note also that the Advertising Code requires that mailing lists should be kept accurate and up to date.

Question: Are there any restrictions on the use of mailing lists, for example, may a list of persons who have previously bought double glazing be used to promote holiday packages?

Answer: The Data Protection Act 1984 requires that data shall be held only for one or more specified and lawful purposes. It further requires that data held for any purpose or purposes shall not be used or disclosed in any manner incompatible with that purpose or those purposes. If the holding of mailing lists on computer has been properly registered with the Data Protection Registrar for trading purposes generally there should be no difficulty about their use for other compatible trading purposes. However, it should always be borne in mind that data collected for a confidential or sensitive purpose ought not to be used for any other purposes. Examples may be lists of debtors, lists of persons buying personal hygiene or contraceptive products and so on.

Question: Can anything be done to prevent the copying of mailing lists?

Answer: The unauthorised copying of mailing lists is theft contrary to the Theft Act 1968. There have been a number of successful private prosecutions for such thefts.

The Data Protection Act 1984 requires that personal data shall be obtained and processed fairly and lawfully. It therefore follows that the Data Protection Registrar could take action against any person who obtained a mailing list unlawfully.

Question: Where can more information be obtained about the Data Protection Act 1984 and its effect on sales promotions?

Answer: The Data Protection Registrar publishes a number of booklets and leaflets on the operation of the Act. He is also willing to advise registered data-holders. He may be reached at the Office of the Data Protection Registrar, Wycliffe House, Water Lane, Wilmslow, Cheshire SK9 5AF.

Chapter 9
BRIBERY AND CORRUPTION

Bribery legislation

Question: What legislation covers this field?

Answer: The Public Bodies Corrupt Practices Act 1889 and the Prevention of Corruption Acts 1906–1916.

Section 1 of The Public Bodies Corrupt Practices Act 1889 makes it an offence where any person by himself or with others:

(a) corruptly solicits or receives or agrees to receive any gift, loan, fee, reward or advantage whatever as an inducement or reward for, or otherwise on account of, any member of a public body or public official or decides not to do something in respect of any matter or transaction with which the relevant public body is concerned;

(b) corruptly gives, promises, or offers any gift, loan, fee, reward or advantage as an inducement or reward for or otherwise on account of any member of a public body or any public official for doing something or deciding not to do something in respect of any matter or transaction with which the relevant public body is concerned.

Question: Why is this legislation a potential problem for promoters?

Answer: The long title of the legislation is given as 'An Act for the more effectual Prevention and Punishment of Bribery and Corruption of and by Members,

Officers, or Servants of Corporations, Councils, Boards, Commissions or other Public Bodies'. The relevance of section 1, which is paraphrased above, is that if a promotional scheme gives rise to corruption, the promoter will be open to prosecution for a criminal offence, as well as the recipient.

Question: How does the Public Bodies Corrupt Practices Act 1889 affect promotions?

Answer: This Act, as its name suggests, is designed to protect the neutrality and impartiality of members of public authorities, officers of public authorities and public servants. This means that no bribes should be made to a public servant. In this regard it is important to note that 'public body' includes public authorities of all kinds, at both local and national level. The Civil Aviation Authority and the Gas Boards have been held to be public bodies but, interestingly, the National Coal Board has been held not to be a public body.

In addition, promoters should be aware that the 1889 Act imposes a presumption that a gift or other consideration has been paid or given and received corruptly, unless the contrary is proved. And the penalties are much higher too in respect of public officials.

Question: What does bribery mean in sales promotion terms?

Answer: Bribery means basically offering an advantage to a public servant, in money or money's worth, which could influence the way he carries out his work, with the result that business favours are secured whch would not otherwise be the case. The fact that it does not influence him does not mean that an offence has not been committed. A charge of attempted bribery could be made. The important public policy consideration is that public servants should be above suspicion. No incentive scheme should be aimed at public servants. In any event, it is likely to be be counter-productive to aim an incentive scheme at public servants because they will invariably have nothing to do with such approaches. Many will even refuse the offer of a free lunch.

Question: Does this apply to public servants in their private capacity?

Answer: No. The problem lies where the incentive is directed to them in their official capacity in a way that influences their judgement in relation to public issues.

Question: What about people other than public servants?

Answer: Apart from the Public Bodies Corrupt Practices Act there are the Prevention of Corruption Acts. Accordingly there can be a problem if a gift or incentive to an individual employee causes, or is a potential cause, of a conflict of interests with his employer. Take a purchasing officer, for example. His duty is to purchase goods with only one consideration; the best interests of his company. If a promoter offers him a canteen of cutlery for purchasing from a particular supplier, then his personal interest and the company's interest may well conflict.

Question: Does the value of the incentive make any difference?

Answer: In practice it does, because if the value is not significant it is unlikely to be sufficient to encourage an employee to disregard his employer's interests. Accordingly, small gifts and similar incentives are probably acceptable but they should be carefully monitored.

Lessening the risk

Question: Is there any action I can take to lessen the risk of trouble?

Answer: Yes. First, it will help considerably if the employer is made aware of the incentive and gives his consent. It is hard to see how an offence would arise if the employer is made aware of the scheme and does not object.

Secondly, the terms of the incentive should state that participation is dependent on the participants having the permission of senior management.

Thirdly, it is important to make sure that the incentive is delivered to the company address and not a private residence.

Fourthly, where possible the incentive should be presented as a corporate benefit rather than an individual one.

Rules and guidance

Question: Are there any notes of guidance on this subject?

Answer: Yes. Both the Chartered Institute of Purchasing and Supply (CIPS) and the Incorporated Society of British Advertisers (ISBA) have produced helpful publications. The CIPS, which is the professional organisation for purchasing officers, has issued 'Rules for Trade Promotions' which have been designed to overcome the legal and ethical difficulties connected with personal incentives. The ISBA, which is the trade association for advertisers, has issued a set of principles of good practice. Both these documents are set out as appendices.

Prosecutions

Question: Who can prosecute?

Answer: For a breach of section 1 a prosecution may only be instituted by or with the agreement of the Attorney-General or the Solicitor-General.

Question: What are the penalties?

Answer: On conviction on indictment at the Crown Court a person is liable to imprisonment for a term not exceeding two years or to a fine or both. Where the offence relates to a contract or proposed contract with Her Majesty, a government department or a public body, the maximum sentence is seven years' imprisonment. In addition, the public official is liable to forfeit the gift, lose his public appointment and be banned from holding any public office for five years.

Sales Promotion Code

Question: Does the British Code of Sales Promotion Practice have anything to say on this?

Answer: Yes. Clause 43 of the Sales Promotion Code sets out a number of important rules. The important principle in the Code is that no trade incentive to employees should be such as to cause any conflict with the duty of employees to their employer, and promoters should normally secure the prior agreement of the employer or responsible manager. Trade incentives should not compromise the obligation of those employees giving advice to the public to give honest advice.

Question: Are there any controls which directly apply to purchasing officers?

Answer: Yes. Members of the Chartered Institute of Purchasing and Supply are required, as a condition of membership, to comply with the Institute's Ethical Code which is designed to ensure that members never use their authority or office for personal gain and continually seek to uphold and enhance the purchasing and supply profession.

Tax

Question: Are there any tax implications?

Answer: An additional concern for promotors devising trade incentive schemes is the tax implications. Regard should be had, for example, to section 577 of the Income and Corporation Taxes Act 1988 which deals with business entertaining expenses.

The terms of the incentive should make clear to participants that there may be a tax liability, and that they should check their position.

Question: What about business gifts?

Answer: Business gifts present the same potential problems as incentives. Again, one must use common sense and consider certain factors, such as the position and remuneration level of the recipient, whether the recipient can provide business favours for the donor, and whether the gift has a business use.

Chapter 10

MISCELLANEOUS LEGAL ISSUES

Trading stamps

Question: I have heard there is legislation on trading stamps. What is it?

Answer: Trading stamps are subject to the Trading Stamps Act 1964 – a piece of legislation which followed the wave of trading stamps schemes in the early 1960s.

Question: What is a trading stamp?

Answer: The Act defines a trading stamp very widely. 'Stamp' is defined as meaning any 'stamp, coupon, voucher, token or similar device, whether adhesive or not, other than lawful money of the realm'. 'Trading stamp' is defined as meaning a stamp 'which is, or is intended to be, delivered to any person upon or in connection with a purchase by that person of any goods (other than a newspaper or other periodical of which the stamp forms part or in which it is contained) and is, or is intended to be, redeemable (whether singly or together with other such stamps) by that or some other person'.

Question: This is a very wide definition. Surely it will cover a number of sales promotion devices?

Answer: Technically, yes. Almost any ticket or voucher given away with the sale of goods which is subsequently redeemable by that person would be a trading stamp. This includes money-off coupons given on pack, such as '10p of next purchase'. It does not, however, cover coupons that are distributed, for example, by a leaflet drop. However, it should be noted that these sort of promotional devices were not in the minds of the Parliamentary draftsmen and, in practice, the law has never been enforced, to the authors' knowledge, in this field. Indeed, the Trading Stamps Act fell very much into abeyance when trading stamps declined as a promotional device.

Question: What consequences flow from a device being a trading stamp?

Answer: The main requirement is that the stamp must carry on its face a cash redemption value in current coin of the realm. This cash redemption value does not have to equate with the value of the coupon if it is redeemed in the way that the promoter envisages. In other words, a coupon with a redemption value of 10p off a subsequent purchase does not need to have a cash redemption value of 10p. It can be any figure one chooses, and is usually a fraction of 1p. In addition, section 7 of the Act requires a display of information in shops where a trading stamp scheme is operated, giving full particulars concerning the stamps and the number of stamps that are necessary in order to finance any particular transaction.

Question: What is the significance of the cash redemption value?

Answer: Under section 3 of the Act, when someone has collected 25p's worth of trading stamps, ie stamps which have a total cash redemption value of 25p, then one can demand a cash redemption.

Question: So many money-off coupons don't carry a cash redemption value. Does it matter?

Answer: My job as author is to tell readers the legal position as I understand it. It cannot be denied, however, that there are certain devices which are technically trading stamps but which rarely, if ever, comply with the Act. Some schemes, such as Air Miles, are not only trading stamps within the technical definition but are clearly within the original concept of trading stamps. Air Miles vouchers do contain a cash redemption value and one would be exceedingly foolish to run a similar scheme and not comply with the Act. The money-off coupons on detergent packets are more problematical. Although it is easy to imprint a cash redemption value on the coupon one also has to comply, as we have seen, with the provisions of section 7 of the Act. On the other hand, some commentators have suggested that in the absence of an official cash redemption value a court might regard the amount which is actually printed on the coupon as the cash redemption value. Given the rights of consumers to encash trading stamps, the implications of this are obvious.

Safety of promotional goods

Question: Are promotional goods subject to the law on consumer safety and if so, what are those laws?

Answer: Yes. The law on consumer safety is now contained in parts I and II of the Consumer Protection Act 1987, which has been extended by the General Product Safety Regulations 1994. That law relates to the 'supply' of dangerous goods and thus goods offered free as incentives are subject to the law. Part I of the Act imposes strict product liability. That means that any person who suffers damage to his or her person or to property can sue the producer of the product for unlimited damages without the need to prove the existence of a contract or negligence. Part II of the Act requires that all consumer goods shall comply with the 'general safety requirement', ie they shall be as safe as may be reasonably expected. Any producer or distributor who supplies goods contrary to the general safety requirement is liable to prosecution.

Question: Who is liable if a person is injured by an incentive product?

Answer: The producer or distributor is liable. Where a retailer offers own-label products he is deemed to be 'holding himself out to be the producer' and is liable unless he makes it clear that the product is supplied to him or manufactured for him.

Question: Who is liable under part II of the Act in respect of the general safety requirement?

Answer: The position is quite different from part I of the Act. Failure to comply with the general safety requirement is a criminal offence and any producer or distributor who supplies consumer goods, or offers or agrees to supply such goods, or exposes or possesses such goods for supply which do not conform to the general safety requirement is liable to prosecution.

Question: What is the general safety requirement?

Answer: Goods are deemed to fail to comply with the requirement if they are not reasonably safe having regard to all the circumstances.

Consumer credit

Question: How does Consumer Credit law control credit linked promotions?

Answer: The Consumer Credit Act 1974 and the regulations made thereunder include strict controls on advertising and other activities seeking business.

The controls are:

(a) it is an offence to advertise goods or services on credit when it is not intended also to offer them for cash;

(b) it is an offence to advertise credit facilities in a manner which is false or misleading in a material respect;

(c) where an advertiser commits one of the offences given above the publisher of the advertisement, any person who devised the advertisement and any person who procured the advertisement are also, subject to certain defences and exemptions, liable to prosecution;

(d) it is an offence to canvass credit business off trade premises;

(e) it is an offence to send a minor any document inviting him to borrow money, obtain goods or services on credit, or to apply for information or advice on borrowing money.

Question: Most credit-linked promotions concern low or no deposit or interest finance. Are there any particular difficulties with this type of promotion?

Answer: Credit advertisements must fit into one of three different categories in each of which there is a minimum, and in all but the full category, a maximum amount of information to be given. The regulations governing credit advertising change from time to time but generally speaking there is no difficulty with low or no deposit and/or interest offers. Professional advice should always be sought on the form and content of credit advertisements, and it should be noted that the Office of Fair Trading has recommended a substantial simplification of the rules on consumer credit advertising.

Origin marking

Question: Must imported promotion goods be marked with an indication of origin?

Answer: The law relating to origin marking is contained in the Trade Descriptions (Place of Production) (Marking) Order 1988. That Order requires that where goods are presented in such a way as to indicate that they were manufactured or produced elsewhere than is the case, they shall be marked with or accompanied by a clear, legible and conspicuous statement as to the place where they were manufactured or produced. Where the indication is likely to create the impression that the goods were produced or manufactured in a country other than that in which they were manufactured or produced that statement must also include a statement of the country where they were in fact manufactured or produced.

Matters to which regard must be had in deciding whether such an impression is created are names, images, emblems, flags, devices, references to or representations of things (including buildings, structures and geographical features) or to or of persons (whether living, dead or fictional).

These requirements apply to goods offered free of charge by way of promotions.

Companies Act 1985

Question: Surely the Companies Act has nothing to tell us on the legality of sales promotion schemes?

Answer: Yes it does. Although the Companies Act cannot be regarded as a mainstream piece of legislation affecting sales promotion, it does have its implications.

A sales promotion scheme may well involve a printed order form, perhaps on a leaflet, on which one can order goods – for example a self-liquidating offer. That order form is therefore subject to section 351 of the Companies Act 1985, which requires certain information to be contained within all letters and order forms of a company. Strange though it may seem, if there is no order form, then the law does not apply. For example, instead of a printed order form one might just say 'Send £2.50 to the address below'.

Question: What information needs to go into a company order form?

Answer: It needs to contain details of the place of registration, registered address and the registered number. And it should be noted that these requirements will cover not just the order form but also any accompanying letter.

Other legislation

Question: In a self-liquidating offer, people do not have the opportunity to inspect the goods before purchase. What effect does that have?

Answer: This means that certain legislation will apply that requires the provision of particular consumer information. For example, the Textile Products (Indications of Fibre Content) Regulations 1986 require details of fibre content to be given on labels attached to a product so that they can be seen before purchase. Obviously, if one is ordering goods on the strength of an advertisement or a promotional leaflet one cannot inspect the goods first. Accordingly, under Regulation 6 one is required to give the information in the advertisement. The Regulation refers to advertisements '... intended for retail customers describing textile products with sufficient particularity to enable the products to be ordered by reference only to the description in the advertisement . . .'

A similar requirement exists under the Trade Descriptions (Sealskin Goods) (Information) Order 1980, under which information must be given with sealskin goods as to the fact that they are sealskin and the country in which the seals were killed. Article 5 applies this requirement to advertisements where there is no possibility of inspecting the goods first.

Finally, the same regime applies to direct response advertisements for nightwear. The Nightwear (Safety) Regulations 1985 require such advertisements to give information about the flammability of the product advertised.

Question: Is there not something called the Mock Auctions Act? Does it have any relevance?

Answer: Yes, the Mock Auctions Act 1961 makes it an offence to conduct a mock auction. This is defined as an auction at which one or more lots is sold to a person for less than the amount of his highest bid, or part of the price is repaid or credited to him. Although it is not enormously important legislation for the sales promotion industry it should be borne in mind, particularly when, for example, an idea for a competition involves bidding for various items.

Charity promotions

Question: Is there any special legislation affecting charity promotions?

Answer: Charity promotions are affected by the Charities Act 1992 and the Charitable Institutions

(Fundraising) Regulations 1995. There are a number of implications for promoters, or commercial participators, as they are styled in the legislation. In any promotion which represents that charitable contributions are to be made, there has to be a clear statement indicating:

(a) the name or names of the institution or institutions concerned;

(b) if there is more than one institution concerned, the proportions in which the institutions are respectively to benefit; and

(c) (in general terms) the method by which it is to be determined – (i) what proportion of the consideration given for goods or services sold or supplied by him, or of any other proceeds of a promotional venture undertaken by him, is to be given to or applied for the benefit of the institution or institutions concerned, or (ii) what sums by way of donations by him in connection with the sale or supply of any such goods or services are to be so given or applied, as the case may require.

The 1995 Regulations require a comprehensive written agreement between the charity and the promoter, covering all aspects of the promotion, including how the charity is to benefit and the obligations of the promoter.

Question: Finally, what about tax and VAT implications?

Answer: Tax is a complicated subject in its own right and it would be outside the scope of this book to deal with it. However, readers may be interested to know that in 1984 the Board of Inland Revenue approved arrangements for collecting tax on non-cash incentive prizes awarded to employees. A note giving further details can be obtained from the Inland Revenue Incentive Valuation Unit, Room 135, New

Wing, Somerset House, London WC2R 1LB (tel: 071-438 7329).

Similarly, VAT is a complex subject in its own right, but it is worth mentioning the case of *Boots Company v Commissioners of Customs and Excise* (1990). The court decided that money-off coupons, obtained by consumers when they buy goods, are not a consideration when they are used to buy other goods. They are simply evidence of entitlement to a discount. Output VAT is therefore due only on the net amount which the consumer actually pays for the goods.

CHAPTER 11

EUROPE

Background

Question: What do people mean by the European Union?

Answer: The Maastricht Treaty, or the Treaty on European Union to give it its formal title, was signed on 7 February 1992, and came into operation on 1 November 1993. As most people know, the Treaty created the European Union and the concept of 'citizen of the Union'. However, contrary to popular view, the 'Union' is not a new name for the EEC, or the European Community.

In fact, the European Union is like an umbrella under which the three original Treaties which make up the European Communities continue. They are the European Coal and Steel Community Treaty, the European Atomic Energy Community Treaty ('Euratom') and, most importantly, the EEC – although the latter has now been renamed the European Community Treaty (EC). The European Union also embraces provisions on cooperation in the fields of justice and home affairs, on a common foreign and security policy and special rules on social policy – although a protocol to the Treaty excludes the UK from this element.

Question: Tell me more about the European Community Treaty.

Answer: The European Community is the successor to the EEC, which it replaced as a result of the Maastricht Treaty. The EC Treaty, which was originally signed in Rome in 1957, is the bedrock of economic intergration within Europe and it contains within it most of the important Treaty provisions that affect business and commerce within Europe. For example, within it are contained the rules on European competition law, and also the fundamental provisions on free movement of persons, goods and capital. And, as we shall see later on, the EC Treaty has also been the basis for the development of the principles on freedom of movement of goods, which became so powerfully expressed in the famous *Cassis de Dijon* case.

Question: What are the institutions of the European Community?

Answer: The European Community shares the same institutions with the two other Communities – Euratom and the European Coal and Steel Community. These institutions are as follows:

1   The Council of Ministers

The Council of Ministers consists of a Government minister from each Member State of the Community. The identity of that minister depends on the subject matter under discussion so that periodically there are meetings, for example, of agriculture ministers, transport ministers and consumer ministers. The chairmanship is taken in turns giving each Member State six months in rotation.

2   The Commission

The Commission is somewhat analagous to the UK civil service in that its functions are to develop proposals and implement agreed Community policies. Twenty commissioners are appointed by the Member States. The big four – the UK, France, Italy and the Federal Republic of Germany – appoint two commissioners each, as indeed does Spain, whilst the others appoint one each. Unlike the Council, where national interests are paramount, the Commission is intended to operate in the interests of the Community as a whole.

Each commissioner has a five year term, which may be renewed, and each assumes responsibility for a particular area, or 'portfolio', of Community business.

3   The Court of Justice of the European Communities

The European Union has its own legal order, arising from the treaties, and it takes precedence over the domestic law of each Member State. The Court of Justice consists of 16 judges and eight advocates-general, and is the final arbiter on matters of European law. Based in Luxembourg, the Court is frequently asked to give 'preliminary rulings' on points of European law referred to it by various national courts.

4   The European Parliament

The role of the Parliament is largely consultative, although its influence has been growing since direct elections. Its 626 members serve for five years and they form their own political groupings. It is based in Luxembourg although it sometimes meets elsewhere, particularly in Brussels where committee meetings are held. Plenary sessions are held in Strasbourg. Amongst other rights, it has the right to be consulted about Community legislation, to question members of the Commission and to reject the Community budget.

5   The Economic and Social Committee

The Economic and Social Committee, based in Brussels, is an advisory body designed to involve representatives of the various economic and social interest groups by giving them a vehicle for the expression of their views. Under the EC Treaty, the Council and the Commission must seek the views of the Committee on a wide range of issues. Membership of the Committee is in three groups: employers (group 1); trade unions (group 2); various interests (group 3).

Commission involvement in marketing

Question: Why did the Commission get involved in the area of marketing?

Answer: There are two reasons why the European Commission is involved in the area of marketing.

First, there was the pressure to give the Community a human face in a Europe that appeared to be characterised by wine lakes and butter mountains. Accordingly, the European Commission launched its first Consumer Action Programme in 1974, and over the years a number of further consumer action programmes have followed. This has led to a number of measures in the consumer protection field which have a major impact on marketing, such as the Directives on Misleading Advertising, Doorstep Selling and Product Liability.

As a result of the Maastricht Treaty, consumer protection has been given a greatly enhanced role, and the Commission's Consumer Policy Service is busy on a number of measures of concern to those in marketing; for example, in the area of consumer guarantees.

Secondly, the involvement of the Commission in the field of marketing is a natural consequence of the whole notion of an economic community, in which there is the progressive elimination of barriers. The push towards 1992 and the completion of the Internal Market involved consideration of barriers to cross-frontier trade and, at the time of writing, the European Commission is working on a Green Paper on Commercial Communications which will examine comprehensively the restrictions that still exist on pan-European marketing in all the relevant marketing disciplines.

European legislation

Question: I understand about Acts of Parliament, but I am confused about the legislation that comes from Brussels and the form it takes.

Answer: There are two main forms of legislation emanating from the European Union. They are Directives and Regulations.

1 EC Directives

Article 189 of the EC Treaty says 'A Directive shall be binding as to the result to be achieved, upon each Member State to which it is addressed, but shall leave to national authorities the choice of form and methods.' The Member States are given a period, usually two years, in which to give effect to the Directive. The European Court has considerably extended the importance of directives so that in certain circumstances individuals can claim damages for their non-implementation.

2 EC Regulations

Article 189 says that 'a Regulation shall have general application. It shall be binding in its entirety and directly applicable in all Member

States.' Unlike a Directive, a Regulation lays down immediate legal obligations throughout the Community. Regulations are usually made where it is necessary to have common European rules, usually on technical issues.

Cassis de Dijon

Question: Much seems to be made of the *Cassis de Dijon* case in the context of European marketing. Why?

Answer: Article 30 of the European Community Treaty is the legal bedrock of free circulation of goods within the Community. It forbids the Member States to institute quantitive restrictions on imports and any measures having equivalent effect. A long line of cases on this Article have arisen in the Court of Justice over the years – the most famous of which is *Cassis de Dijon.*

The *Cassis* case involved the famous French blackcurrent liqueur. As produced in France, it contained 15-20% alcohol by volume. Problems arose in relation to its importation into Germany, because German law required such a product to have at least 32% alcohol. It could be imported into Germany, but it was not possible to market it as 'Creme de Cassis'.

The European Court held that such indirect discrimination fell foul of Article 30 and, since the German rule could not be justified on other grounds, it was contrary to the Treaty. Accordingly, the case opened up the markets of Europe to cross-frontier trade, even where the national marketing restrictions applied to imports and domestic industry alike. Henceforward, national restrictions which had the effect of denying goods access to a particular national market had to be justified, and had to be abandoned in the absence of such justification.

The European sales promotion scene

Question: Is it correct to say that national rules in the UK on sales promotion are the most liberal in Europe?

Answer: Yes – although Ireland's rules are very similar.

Germany has the most restrictive rules affecting sales promotion. For example, premiums are allowed only if a reasonable price is charged, or the premium is of insiginificant value, or it can be regarded as a product accessory.

Other European Union countries have serious restrictions on promotions. For example, France has limits on the value of premiums – 7% of the selling price of the purchased article. Free draws and instant win mechanics are not allowed in Germany, Denmark and the Benelux countries. Money-off next purchase is not allowed in Germany, Denmark and Luxembourg.

Generally speaking, the more northerly countries are more restrictive than the southerly ones. Those countries like Germany, which heavily restrict sales promotion, do so because they believe that promotional techniques have the effect of deflecting the consumer's attention from rational purchasing decisions based on an objective analysis of a product's characteristics. A basic checklist of restrictions throughout Europe is set out as an appendix, but readers need to make their own checks as circumstances change.

Question: How do I go about checking a promotion in other European countries?

Answer: As we have seen, the national rules on sales promotion vary considerably across the European Union, and in order to run a pan-European promotion one would need to check out the position in each individual country. To a degree, one can do this through research of written materials in the UK, since there are a number of summaries which detail the basic restrictions on a country-to-country basis.

However, there is no substitute for detailed advice about the current restrictions in each country and, more particularly, the way in which they are applied in practice. In order to achieve this sort of advice, one needs to take professional opinion directly from practitioners in the various countries concerned. If this is not possible, then an alternative is to make use of one of the networks of marketing lawyers that are retained by a small number of London law firms. Quite a number of law firms have European and international networks, but in the area of sales promotion it is important to have access to a network of lawyers who are experienced in this particular area of legal practice.

European self-regulation

Question: Does self-regulation operate across Europe?

Answer: Self-regulation in Europe operates principally on the basis of national systems and national codes. There is a great deal of similarity between these codes, not least because they owe much of their inspiration to the Codes of Marketing Practice produced by the International Chamber of Commerce (ICC).

However, a measure of co-ordination has been achieved through the establishment of the European Advertising Standards Alliance (EASA).

The EASA brings together the advertising self-regulatory bodies from 15 European Community and European Free Trade Association countries. Through the EASA has developed a system that makes it possible for consumers to complain about a cross-border advertisement or sales promotion simply by writing to the complainant's own national advertising self-regulatory body, such as the ASA in the UK.

If the complaint turns out to be a cross-border complaint, it is passed to the relevant self-regulatory body in the country of origin of the medium in which the advertisement appeared. It is then checked for compliance with the rules set out in that country's code of advertising and/or sales promotion practice.

Chapter 12
ADMINISTRATION CHECKLIST

There is an old saying that a chain is as strong as its weakest link. Nowhere is this more true than in the world of sales promotion. A lot of links in the chain have to hang together effectively for a promotion to be a success. So many of the sales promotion schemes that feature in the case reports of the Advertising Standards Authority are not the result of a failure by the promoter and its agency to appreciate the law and the codes; rather they are the result of various failures of administration.

Another thought to concentrate the mind is that the cost of a failure of administration can be truly colossal. Potentially, a promotion that goes wrong can be much more expensive to a company than an advertising campaign which goes wrong. As someone put it to me recently, 'The ending of a promotion can require just as much thought as the beginning of one.'

Accordingly, in the sales promotion law conferences that I organise, I make sure there is a session on administration in which we can examine the practical problems that can arise in the running of a promotion. This book is not the place for a detailed consideration of such issues, but I have taken the opportunity to set out a checklist of some of the major issues affecting the administration of a promotion. From experience, I know how crucial such issues are to a promotion's success.

1   *Taking sales promotion seriously:* Within marketing departments of major companies, there has been a tendency to regard sales promotion as the Cinderella of the marketing mix. Some years ago, an advertising agency executive said to me that, whereas sales promotion was a mechanical operation, advertising was a cerebral activity. This snobbish view about the role of sales promotion means that decisions relating to sales promotion have all too often not been taken at a senior enough level within the company, and this in itself can lead to problems of administration.

Fortunately, the growth of sales promotion as a marketing discipline has necessitated a re-evaluation of its importance by other marketing disciplines, and by those in the marketing departments of major companies. This is crucial, as one of the prime considerations in sales promotion schemes being effective is that companies take sales promotion as a marketing discipline as seriously as they do advertising and other marketing disciplines.

2   *Outside suppliers:* Inevitably, promoters frequently need to use outside suppliers in order to fulfil the needs of a promotion, whether it is a sourcing company, a travel company, or a handling house. It is crucial that the promoter makes sure that the outside companies that they use to fulfil the promotion are up to the job. Many promoters take little interest in the standing and position of outside suppliers, or with supervising their work, with the result that the reputation of the promoter itself suffers.

The promoter must institute appropriate checks into the standing and effectiveness of the outside companies that they use and, in appropriate cases, they should use only those companies that are members of an association which have a recognised code of practice. For example, in the case of handling houses it is important that promoters use only those companies that are members of the Promotional Handling Association and are, therefore, subject to the code of practice for promotional handling houses.

3   *Contracts:* In order to run a successful promotion, a great many relationships need to function effectively. And this is where careful drafting of contracts becomes important. Apart from the contract between agency and promoter, there will be many others with those who are responsible for fulfilling the promotion, such as printers, sourcing companies and handling houses. Contractual issues have already been touched on earlier in this book, but particularly important are the fundamental questions of who does what and when. Issues of quality are also fundamental, particularly in contracts with sourcing companies.

There are, of course, many other issues to consider but the fundamental point is that the good administration of a promotion requires clear and comprehensive contracts.

4. *Effective communication:* Time and time again, a promotion fails and falls foul of the British Code of Sales Promotion because of inadequate briefing. It is no good for the marketing department to be clear in their own mind what needs to happen for a promotion to be legally sound and in compliance with the codes, if the people who need to operate the promotion properly down the line are not clearly briefed. For example, bar staff who should be handing out instant win cards irrespective of purchase fail to do so because they have not been adequately briefed. Effective communication and briefing of all those involved in a promotion is therefore crucial.

5. *Careful estimations:* A successful promotion requires a careful estimate of likely consumer demand from the promotion, and proper arrangements to meet that demand. This is by far one of the most important administrative aspects of running a promotion. Indeed, the British Code of Sales Promotion requires promoters to make a reasonably pre-estimate of likely demand. This is not just a Code requirement; it is also a commercial necessity.

6. *Realistic budgets:* Akin to making a careful estimate of likely demand is to make sure the budget for the promotion is adequate to the likely demand.

7. *Realistic timetables:* So often, unrealistic timetables are included within a promotion. This is particularly true of competitions which involve a lengthy judging process. A timetable for judging and award of prizes needs to be instituted, and not infrequently this cannot be met and, therefore, there is a problem of slippage of dates. It is crucial that realistic dates are set for a promotion, ie dates that the promoter knows can be complied with, and which make allowances for absences and the natural delaying factors which arise in everyday life.

8   *Check and double-check:* So many promotions have come adrift over the years because assumptions have been made, particularly assumptions that other people have done what is required of them.

It is important for promoters to check and re-check almost everything to do with a promotion to make sure that everything that should happen, does happen, and that everybody who has a role to play meets their obligations. Some of the worst catastrophes in sales promotion have arisen because assumptions have been made, particularly assumptions that people can be relied on, when they cannot.

9   *Complaints:* Dealing with complaints in respect of the promotion are an important challenge for promoters. One should always deal positively with complaints, whether they are justified or unjustified. There is nothing worse than a weak and vascillating response.

If the complaint is justified, then by far the best way to defuse the issue is to apologise and make an appropriate gesture of amends. Nothing keeps an issue alive more effectively than for a company to prevaricate and make excuses when it is patently obvious to an independent observer that some mistake has been made and the company is trying to cover up. At the end of the day, the company gains more credit from an open acknowledgement and apology.

If, on the other hand, the complaint is groundless, then it is important that a firm and resolute response is given, and important that no token is given which could be interpreted as an acknowledgement of weakness on the part of the promoter. If the promoter's position is sound, then the promoter must stand firm.

10   *Keep records:* There is a growing number of professional competition addicts, known in the trade as 'compers'. Some are prepared to challenge the adjudication on competitions – in some cases several years after the competition has been run. In addition, there are growing numbers of people prepared to challenge the way in which promotions are organised and administered.

In order to deal properly with these challenges, a promoter must keep proper records and for a reasonable period of time. It is difficult to say what that period should be, but in my view it should be at least three years.

11 *Checklist:* It is important for those in the sales promotion industry to develop their own checklists in order to ensure a systematic approach to the creation, planning and administration of each promotion. The issues we have discussed here should provide a basis for such a checklist.

12 *'The secretary test':* Those who give professional advice about promotions know only too well that the most valuable service that can be rendered in respect of a promotion is often the provision of an independent view. We often cannot see clearly something that we are closely involved in, and we need an independent third party to look at what we are doing.

Accordingly, there is much to be said for getting such an independent person to read through the material for a promotion, because he or she can look at a promotion very much through the eyes of an ordinary consumer, without the involved knowledge and experience of those who put the promotion together. So often, agencies and promoters have persuaded themselves that a particular piece of wording is clear, when the moment that material is seen by a third party it is patently obvious that it is far from clear, and highly ambiguous, to say the least.

That independent third party can be anybody, but I call this test 'the secretary test' because secretaries are often blessed with a considerable degree of commonsense and this makes them peculiarly well-suited to giving an independent view about the wording and presentation of a promotion.

APPENDICES

Appendix		
1	The British Codes of Advertising and Sales Promotion	113
2	Code of Practice for Traders on Price Indications	168
3	Notes for Guidance on Coupons – Recommended Best Practice	191
4	The Institute of Sales Promotion: Promotional Handling Code of Practice	198
5	Incorporated Society of British Advertisers: Trade Incentives – Good and Bad Practice	211
6	The Chartered Institute of Purchasing and Supply: Ethical Code	214
7	The Chartered Institute of Purchasing and Supply: Rules for Trade Promotions	217
8	Checklist of Restrictions on Sales Promotion Activities in Individual European Countries	219
9	Useful Addresses	222

APPENDICES

Appendix 1
THE BRITISH CODES OF ADVERTISING AND SALES PROMOTION

Published February 1995

Published by, and reproduced here with the permission of, The Committee of Advertising Practice, Brook House, Torrington Place, London WC7E 7HW, Tel: 0171–580 5555; Fax: 0171–631 3051

The Committee of Advertising Practice is the self-regulatory body that devises and enforces the Codes. CAP's members include organisations that represent the advertising, sales promotion and media businesses.

The Advertising Standards Authority is the independent body responsible for ensuring that the system works in the public interest. The ASA's activities include investigating complaints and conducting research.

For fast, free and confidential copy advice on your advertising and promotions, tel 0171–580 4100 or fax 0171–580 4072.

Members of The Committee of Advertising Practice

Advertising Association
Association of Household Distributors
Association of Media and Communications Specialists
Broadcast Advertising Clearance Centre
Cinema Advertising Association
Council of Outdoor Specialists
Direct Mail Services Standards Board
Direct Marketing Association (UK)
Direct Selling Association
Incorporated Society of British Advertisers
Institute of Practitioners in Advertising
Institute of Sales Promotion
Mail Order Traders Association
Mailing Preference Service
Newspaper Publishers Association
Newspaper Society
Outdoor Advertising Association
Periodical Publishers Association
Proprietary Association of Great Britain
Royal Mail
Scottish Daily Newspaper Society
Scottish Newspaper Publishers Association

COMMENCEMENT

This ninth edition of the Advertising Code and sixth edition of the Sales Promotion Code come into force on 1st February 1995. They replace all previous editions.

Contents

CAP Members   114

Introduction   116

Advertising Code   118

Sales Promotion Code   126

Specific Rules   136

Cigarette Code   154

Legislation   158

How the System Works   160

Introduction

1.1 The Codes apply to:

a advertisements in newspapers, magazines, brochures, leaflets, circulars, mailings, catalogues and other printed publications, facsimile transmissions, posters and aerial announcements

b cinema and video commercials

c advertisements in non-broadcast electronic media such as computer games

d viewdata services

e mailing lists except for business-to-business

f sales promotions

g advertisement promotions

h advertisements and promotions covered by the Cigarette Code.

1.2 The Codes do not apply to:

a broadcast commercials, which are the responsibility of the Independent Television Commission or the Radio Authority

b the contents of premium rate telephone calls, which are the responsibility of the Independent Committee for the Supervision of Standards of Telephone Information Services

c advertisements in foreign media

d health-related claims in advertisements and promotions addressed only to the medical and allied professions

e classified private advertisements

f statutory, public, police and other official notices

g works of art exhibited in public or private

h private correspondence

i oral communications, including telephone calls

j press releases and other public relations material

k the content of books and editorial communications

l regular competitions such as crosswords

m flyposting

n packages, wrappers, labels and tickets unless they advertise a sales promotion or are visible in an advertisement

o point of sale displays except for those covered by the Sales Promotion Code and the Cigarette Code

1.3 The following definitions apply to the Codes:

a a *product* encompasses goods, services, ideas, causes or opportunities, prizes and gifts

b a *consumer* is anyone who is likely to see a given advertisement or promotion

c the *United Kingdom* rules cover the Isle of Man and the Channel Islands (except for the purposes of the Cigarette Code)

d a *claim* can be implied or direct, written, spoken or visual

e the Codes are divided into numbered *clauses*

1.4 The following criteria apply to the Codes:

a the judgement of the ASA Council on interpretation of the Codes is final

b conformity is assessed according to the advertisement's probable impact when taken as a whole and in context. This will depend on the audience, the medium, the nature of the product and any additional material distributed at the same time to consumers

c   the Codes are indivisible; advertisers must conform with all appropriate rules

d   the Codes do not have the force of law and their interpretation will reflect their flexibility. The general law operates alongside the Codes; the courts may also make rulings against matters covered by the Codes

e   an indication of the statutory rules governing advertising and promotions is given in the Legislation section; professional advice should be taken if there is any doubt about their application

f   no spoken or written communications with the ASA or CAP should be understood as containing legal advice

g   the Codes are primarily concerned with advertisements and promotions and not with terms of business, products themselves or other contractual matters

h   the rules make due allowance for public sensitivities but will not be used by the ASA to diminish freedom of speech

i   the ASA may decide that it is not qualified to judge advertisements and promotions in languages other than English

j   the ASA does not act as an arbitrator between conflicting ideologies

Advertising Code

Principles

2.1 All advertisements should be legal, decent, honest and truthful.

2.2 All advertisements should be prepared with a sense of responsibility to consumers and to society.

2.3 All advertisements should respect the principles of fair competition generally accepted in business.

2.4 No advertisement should bring advertising into disrepute.

2.5 Advertisements must conform with the Codes. Primary responsibility for observing the Codes falls on advertisers. Others involved in preparing and publishing advertisements such as agencies, publishers and other service suppliers also accept an obligation to abide by the Codes.

2.6 Any unreasonable delay in responding to the ASA's enquiries may be considered a breach of the Codes.

2.7 The ASA will on request treat in confidence any private or secret material supplied unless the courts or officials acting within their statutory powers compel its disclosure.

2.8 The Codes are applied in the spirit as well as in the letter.

Substantiation

3.1 Before submitting an advertisement for publication, advertisers must hold documentary evidence to prove all claims, whether direct or implied, that are capable of objective substantiation. Relevant evidence should be sent without delay if requested by the ASA. The adequacy of evidence will be judged on whether it supports both the detailed claims and the overall impression created by the advertisement.

3.2 If there is a significant division of informed opinion about any claims made in an advertisement they should not be portrayed as universally agreed.

3.3 If the contents of non-fiction books, tapes, videos and the like have not been independently substantiated, advertisements should not exaggerate the value or practical usefulness of their contents.

3.4 Obvious untruths or exaggerations that are unlikely to mislead and incidental minor errors and unorthodox spellings are all allowed provided they do not affect the accuracy or perception of the advertisement in any material way.

Legality

4.1 Advertisers have primary responsibility for ensuring that their advertisements are legal. Advertisements should contain nothing that breaks the law or incites anyone to break it, and should omit nothing that the law requires.

Decency

5.1 Advertisements should contain nothing that is likely to cause serious or widespread offence. Particular care should be taken to avoid causing offence on the grounds of race, religion, sex, sexual orientation or disability. Compliance with the Codes will be judged on the context, medium, audience, product and prevailing standards of decency.

5.2 Advertisements may be distasteful without necessarily conflicting with 5.1 above. Advertisers are urged to consider public sensitivities before using potentially offensive material.

5.3 The fact that a particular product is offensive to some people is not sufficient grounds for objecting to an advertisement for it.

Honesty

6.1 Advertisers should not exploit the credulity, lack of knowledge or inexperience of consumers.

Truthfulness

7.1 No advertisement should mislead by inaccuracy, ambiguity, exaggeration, omission or otherwise.

Matters of opinion

8.1 Advertisers may give a view about any matter, including the qualities or desirability of their products, provided it is clear that they are expressing their own opinion rather than stating a fact. Assertions or comparisons that go beyond subjective opinions are subject to 3.1 above.

Fear and distress

9.1 No advertisement should cause fear or distress without good reason. Advertisers should not use shocking claims or images merely to attract attention.

9.2 Advertisers may use an appeal to fear to encourage prudent behaviour or to discourage dangerous or ill-advised actions; the fear likely to be aroused should not be disproportionate to the risk.

Safety

10.1 Advertisements should not show or encourage unsafe practices except in the context of promoting safety. Particular care should be taken with advertisements addressed to or depicting children and young people.

10.2 Consumers should not be encouraged to drink and drive. Advertisements, including those for breath testing devices, should not suggest that the effects of drinking alcohol can be masked and should include a prominent warning on the dangers of drinking and driving.

Violence and anti-social behaviour

11.1 Advertisements should contain nothing that condones or is likely to provoke violence or anti-social behaviour.

Political advertising

12.1 Any advertisement whose principal function is to influence opinion in favour of or against any political party or electoral candidate contesting a UK, European parliamentary or local government election, or any matter before the electorate for a referendum, is exempt from clauses 3.1, 7.1, 14.3, 19.2 and 20.1. All other rules in the Codes apply.

12.2 The identity and status of such advertisers should be clear. If their address or other contact details are not generally available they should be included in the advertisement.

12.3 There is a formal distinction between government policy and that of political parties. Advertisements by central or local government, or those concerning government policy as distinct from party policy, are subject to all the Codes' rules.

Protection of privacy

13.1 Advertisers are urged to obtain written permission in advance if they portray or refer to individuals or their identifiable possessions in any advertisement. Exceptions include most crowd scenes, portraying anyone who is the subject of the book or film being advertised and depicting property in general outdoor locations.

13.2 Advertisers who have not obtained prior permission from entertainers, politicians, sportsmen and others whose work gives them a high public profile should ensure that they are not portrayed in an offensive or adverse way. Advertisements should not claim or imply an endorsement where none exists.

13.3 Prior permission may not be needed when the advertisement contains nothing that is inconsistent with the position or views of the person featured. Advertisers should be aware that individuals who do not wish to be associated with the advertised product may have a legal claim.

13.4 References to anyone who is deceased should be handled with particular care to avoid causing offence or distress.

13.5 References to members of the Royal Family and the use of the Royal Arms and Emblems are not normally permitted; advertisers should consult the Lord Chamberlain's Office. References to Royal Warrants should be checked with the Royal Warrant Holders' Association.

Testimonials and endorsements

14.1 Advertisers should hold signed and dated proof, including a contact address, for any testimonial they use. Testimonials should be used only with the written permission of those giving them.

14.2 Testimonials should relate to the product being advertised.

14.3 Testimonials alone do not constitute substantiation and the opinions expressed in them must be supported, where necessary, with independent evidence of their accuracy. Any claims based on a testimonial must conform with the Codes.

14.4 Fictitious endorsements should not be presented as though they were genuine testimonials.

14.5 References to tests, trials, professional endorsements, research facilities and professional journals should be used only with the permission of those concerned. They should originate from within the European Union unless otherwise stated in the advertisement. Any establishment referred to should be under the direct supervision of an appropriately qualified professional.

Prices

15.1 Any stated price should be clear and should relate to the product advertised. Advertisers should ensure that prices match the products illustrated.

15.2 Unless addressed exclusively to the trade, prices quoted should include any VAT payable. It should be apparent immediately whether any prices quoted exclude other taxes, duties or compulsory charges and these should, wherever possible, be given in the advertisement.

15.3 If the price of one product is dependent on the purchase of another, the extent of any commitment by consumers should be made clear.

15.4 Price claims such as 'up to' and 'from' should not exaggerate the availability of benefits likely to be obtained by consumers.

Free offers

16.1 There is no objection to making a free offer conditional on the purchase of other items. Consumers' liability for any costs should be made clear in all material featuring the offer. An offer should only be described as free if consumers pay no more than:

a   the current public rates of postage

b   the actual cost of freight or delivery

c   the cost, including incidental expenses, of any travel involved if consumers collect the offer.

Advertisers should make no additional charges for packing and handling.

16.2 Advertisers must not attempt to recover their costs by reducing the quality or composition or by inflating the price of any product that must be purchased as a pre-condition of obtaining another product free.

Availability of products

17.1 Advertisers must make it clear if stocks are limited. Products must not be advertised unless advertisers can demonstrate that they have reasonable grounds for believing that they can satisfy demand. If a product becomes unavailable, advertisers will be required to show evidence of stock monitoring, communications with outlets and the swift withdrawal of advertisements whenever possible.

17.2 Products which cannot be supplied should not normally be advertised as a way of assessing potential demand.

17.3 Advertisers must not use the technique of switch selling, where their sales staff criticise the advertised product or suggest that it is not available and recommend the purchase of a more expensive alternative. They should not place obstacles in the way of purchasing the product or delivering it promptly.

Guarantees

18.1 The full terms of any guarantee should be available for consumers to inspect before they are committed to purchase. Any substantial limitations should be spelled out in the advertisement.

18.2 Advertisers should inform consumers about the nature and extent of any additional rights provided by the guarantee, over and above those given to them by law, and should make clear how to obtain redress.

18.3 'Guarantee' when used simply as a figure of speech should not cause confusion about consumers' legal rights.

Comparisons

19.1 Comparisons can be explicit or implied and can relate to advertisers' own products or to those of their competitors; they are permitted in the interests of vigorous competition and public information.

19.2 Comparisons should be clear and fair. The elements of any comparison should not be selected in a way that gives the advertisers an artificial advantage.

Denigration

20.1 Advertisers should not unfairly attack or discredit other businesses or their products.

20.2 The only acceptable use of another business's broken or defaced products in advertisements is in the illustration of comparative tests, and the source, nature and results of these should be clear.

Exploitation of goodwill

21.1 Advertisers should not make unfair use of the goodwill attached to the trade mark, name, brand, or the advertising campaign of any other business.

Imitation

22.1 No advertisement should so closely resemble any other that it misleads or causes confusion.

Identifying advertisers and recognising advertisements

23.1 Advertisers, publishers and owners of other media should ensure that advertisements are designed and presented in such a way that they can be easily distinguished from editorial.

23.2 Features, announcements or promotions that are disseminated in exchange for a payment or other reciprocal arrangement should comply with the Codes if their content is controlled by the advertisers. They should also be clearly identified and distinguished from editorial (see clause 41).

23.3 Mail order and direct response advertisements and those for one-day sales, homework schemes, business opportunities and the like should contain the name and address of the advertisers. Advertisements with a political content should clearly identify their source. Unless required by law, other advertisers are not obliged to identify themselves.

Sales Promotion Code

Introduction

26.1 The Sales Promotion Code should be read, where appropriate, in conjunction with the rules in the Advertising and Cigarette Codes. The Specific Rules and the sections headed Introduction, Legislation and How the System Works are common to both Codes.

26.2 The Sales Promotion Code is designed primarily to protect the public but it also applies to trade promotions and incentive schemes and to the promotional elements of sponsorships.

26.3 The Sales Promotion Code regulates the nature and administration of promotional marketing techniques. These techniques generally involve providing a range of direct or indirect additional benefits, usually on a temporary basis, designed to make goods or services more attractive to purchasers.

Principles

27.1 All sales promotions should be legal, decent, honest and truthful.

27.2 All sales promotions should be prepared with a sense of responsibility to consumers and to society; they should be conducted equitably, promptly and efficiently and should be seen to deal fairly and honourably with consumers. Promoters should avoid causing unnecessary disappointment.

27.3 All sales promotions should respect the principles of fair competition generally accepted in business.

27.4 No promoter or intermediary should bring sales promotion into disrepute.

27.5 Sales promotions must conform with the Codes. Primary responsibility for observing the Codes falls on promoters. Intermediaries and agents also accept an obligation to abide by the Codes.

27.6 Any unreasonable delay in responding to the ASA's enquiries may be considered a breach of the Codes.

27.7 The ASA will on request treat in confidence any private or secret material supplied unless the courts or officials acting within their statutory powers compel its disclosure.

27.8 The Codes are applied in the spirit as well as in the letter.

Public interest

28.1 Sales promotions should not be designed or conducted in a way that conflicts with the public interest. They should contain nothing that condones or is likely to provoke violent or anti-social behaviour, nuisance, personal injury or damage to property.

Substantiation

29.1 Promoters must be able to demonstrate that they have complied with the Codes by submitting documentary evidence without delay when asked by the ASA. The adequacy of evidence will be judged on whether it supports the detailed claims, on the way in which the sales promotion is administered and on the overall impression created by the promotion.

Legality

30.1 Promoters have primary responsibility for ensuring that what they do is legal. Sales promotions should contain nothing that breaks the law or incites anyone to break it, and should omit nothing that the law requires.

Honesty

31.1 Promoters should not abuse consumers' trust or exploit their lack of knowledge or experience.

Truthfulness

32.1 No sales promotion should mislead by inaccuracy, ambiguity, exaggeration, omission or otherwise.

Protection of consumers and promoters

33.1 Promotions involving adventurous activities should be made as safe as possible by the promoters. Every effort should be made to avoid harming consumers when distributing product samples. Special care should be taken when sales promotions are addressed to children or when products intended for adults may fall into the hands of children. Literature accompanying promotional items should give any necessary safety warnings.

33.2 Promotions should be designed and conducted in a way that respects the right of consumers to a reasonable degree of privacy and freedom from annoyance.

33.3 Consumers should be told before entry if participants may be required to become involved in any of the promoters' publicity or advertising, whether it is connected with the sales promotion or not. Prizewinners should not be compromised by the publication of excessively detailed information.

33.4 Promoters and others responsible for administering sales promotions should ensure that the way they compile and use lists containing personal information about consumers conforms to the Specific Rules on List and Database Practice.

Suitability

34.1 Promoters should make every effort to ensure that unsuitable or inappropriate material does not reach consumers. Neither the sales promotions themselves nor the promotional items should cause offence. Promotions should not be socially undesirable to the audience addressed by encouraging either excessive consumption or inappropriate use.

34.2 Alcoholic drinks and tobacco products should not feature in sales promotions addressed to people who are under eighteen and tobacco promotions should be addressed only to existing smokers (see Cigarette Code and Specific Rules on Alcoholic drinks).

Availability

35.1 Promoters should be able to demonstrate that they have made a reasonable estimate of likely response and that they are capable of meeting that response. This applies in all cases except prize promotions, where the number of prizes available to be awarded should be made clear to participants.

35.2 Phrases such as 'subject to availability' do not relieve promoters of the obligation to take all reasonable steps to avoid disappointing participants.

35.3 If promoters are unable to supply demand for a promotional offer because of any unexpectedly high response or some other unanticipated factor outside their control, products of a similar or greater quality and value or a cash payment should normally be substituted.

Children

36.1 For the purposes of this Code, a child or young person is someone under the age of sixteen. Where appropriate, sales promotions should conform with the Specific Rules on Children.

Participation

37.1 Sales promotions should specify:

a   how to participate, including any conditions and costs

b   the promoters' full name and business address in a form that can be retained by consumers

c   a prominent closing date if applicable; where the final date for purchase of the promoted product differs from the closing date for the submission of claims or entries, this should be made clear to participants

d   any proof of purchase requirements; this information should be emphasised for example by using bold type, separating it from other text or using a different colour

e   where it is not obvious, if there is likely to be a limitation on the availability of promotional packs in relation to any stated closing date of the offer

f   where applicable, geographical or personal restrictions, including whether permission is needed from an adult

g   any other factor likely to influence consumers' decisions or understanding about the promotion

h   that any deadline for responding to an undated mailing will be calculated from the date the mailing was received by consumers.

Administration

38.1   Sales promotions should be conducted under proper supervision and adequate resources should be made available to administer them. Promoters and intermediaries should not give consumers any justifiable grounds for complaint.

38.2   Promoters should allow ample time for each phase of the promotion: notifying the trade, distributing the goods, issuing rules where appropriate, collecting wrappers and the like, judging and announcing the results.

38.3 Promoters should fulfil applications within thirty days unless:

a participants have been told in advance that it is impractical to do so

b participants are informed promptly of unforeseen delays and are offered another delivery date or an opportunity to recover any money paid for the offer.

38.4 When damaged or faulty goods are received by consumers, promoters should ensure that they are either replaced without delay or that a refund is sent immediately. The full cost of replacing damaged or faulty goods should fall on promoters. If an applicant does not receive goods, promoters should normally replace them free of charge.

Free offers and promotions where consumers pay

39.1 In the case of free offers and offers where a payment is required, consumers should be informed if any other conditions apply.

39.2 There is no objection to making a free offer conditional on the purchase of other items. Consumers' liability for any costs should be made clear in all material featuring the offer. An offer should only be described as free if consumers pay no more than:

a the current public rates of postage

b the actual cost of freight or delivery

c the cost, including incidental expenses, of any travel involved if consumers collect the offer.

Promoters should make no additional charges for packing and handling.

39.3 Promoters must not attempt to recover their costs by reducing the quality or composition or by inflating the price of any product that must be purchased as a pre-condition of obtaining a free item.

39.4 Promoters should provide a cash refund, postal order or personal cheque promptly to consumers participating in 'try me free' offers or those with a money-back guarantee.

Promotions with prizes

40.1 Promotions with prizes including competitions, free draws and instant win offers are subject to legal restrictions. Promoters should take legal advice before embarking on such schemes.

40.2 Before making a purchase, participants should be informed of:

a   the closing date for receipt of entries

b   any geographical or personal restrictions such as location or age

c   any requirements for proof of purchase

d   the need to obtain permission to enter from an adult or employer

e   the nature of any prizes

40.3 Before entry, participants should be informed:

a   of any restrictions on the number of entries or prizes

b   if a cash alternative can be substituted for any prize

c   how and when winners will be notified of results

d   how and when winners and results will be announced

e   of the criteria for judging entries

f   where appropriate, who owns the copyright of the entries

g   whether and how entries will be returned by promoters

h   of any intention to use winners in post-event publicity

40.4 Complex rules should be avoided and promoters should not need to supplement conditions of entry with additional rules. If further rules cannot be avoided, participants should be informed how to obtain them; the rules should contain nothing that would have influenced consumers against making a purchase or participating. Participants should always be able to retain entry instructions and rules.

40.5 The closing date for entry to a prize promotion should not be changed unless circumstances outside the reasonable control of the promoters make it unavoidable.

40.6 A poor response or an inferior quality of entries is not an acceptable basis for extending the duration of a promotion or withholding prizes unless the promoters have announced their intention to do so at the outset.

40.7 Promoters must either publish or make available on request details of the name and county of major prizewinners and their winning entries. They should make clear in promotional material how this will be done.

40.8 Unless otherwise stated in advance, prizewinners should receive their prizes no more than six weeks after the promotion has ended.

40.9 If the selection of winning entries is open to subjective interpretation, an independent judge, or a panel including one member who is independent of the competition's promoters and intermediaries, should be appointed. Those appointed to act as judges should be competent to judge the subject matter of the competition. The identity of judges should be made available on request.

40.10 Promoters should ensure that tokens, tickets or numbers for instant win and similar promotions are allocated on a fair and random basis. An independent observer should supervise prize draws to ensure that participants have an equal opportunity of winning.

40.11 Participants in instant win promotions should get their winnings at once or should know immediately what they have won and how to claim it without delay, unreasonable costs or administrative barriers.

40.12 When prize promotions are widely advertised, promoters should ensure that entry forms and any goods needed to establish proof of purchase are widely available.

40.13 The distinction between a prize and a gift should always be clear to consumers. Gifts offered to all or most participants in a promotion should not be described as prizes. If promoters offer a gift to all entrants in addition to giving a prize to those who win, particular care is needed to avoid confusing the two.

40.14 Promoters should avoid exaggerating the likelihood of consumers winning a prize.

Advertisement promotions

41.1 Advertisement promotions should be designed and presented in such a way that they can be easily distinguished from editorial.

41.2 Features, announcements or promotions that are disseminated in exchange for a payment or other reciprocal arrangement should comply with the Codes if their content is controlled by the promoters.

41.3 Publishers announcing reader promotions on the front page or cover should ensure that consumers know whether they will be expected to buy subsequent editions of the publication. Major qualifications that may influence consumers significantly in their decision to purchase the publication should appear on the front page or cover.

Charity-linked promotions

42.1 Promotions claiming that participation will benefit registered charities or good causes should:

a   name each charity or good cause that will benefit, and be able to demonstrate to the ASA that those benefiting consent to the advertising or promotion

b   when it is not a registered charity, define its nature and objectives c   specify exactly what will be gained by the named charity or cause and state the basis on which the contribution will be calculated

d   state if the promoters have imposed any limitations on the contribution they will make out of their own pocket

e   not limit consumers' contributions; any extra money collected should be given to the named charity or cause on the same basis as contributions below that level

f   not exaggerate the benefit to the charity or cause derived from individual purchases of the promoted product

g   if asked, make available to consumers a current or final total of contributions made

h   take particular care when appealing to children (see clause 47.4e).

Trade incentives

43.1   Incentive schemes should be designed and implemented to take account of the interests of everyone involved and should not compromise the obligation of employees to give honest advice to consumers.

43.2   Promoters should secure the prior agreement of employers or of the manager responsible if they intend to ask for assistance from, or offer incentives to, any other company's employees. Promoters should observe any procedures established by companies for their employees, including any rules for participating in promotions. In the case of a trade incentive scheme that has been generally advertised rather than individually targeted, employees should be asked to obtain their employer's permission before participating.

43.3   It should be made clear to those benefiting from an incentive scheme that they may be liable for tax.

Specific Rules

Alcoholic drinks

46.1 For the purposes of the Codes, alcoholic drinks are those that exceed 1.2% alcohol by volume.

46.2 The drinks industry and the advertising business accept a responsibility for ensuring that advertisements contain nothing that is likely to lead people to adopt styles of drinking that are unwise. The consumption of alcohol may be portrayed as sociable and thirst-quenching. Advertisements may be humorous, but must still conform with the intention of the rules.

46.3 Advertisements should be socially responsible and should not encourage excessive drinking. Advertisements should not suggest that regular solitary drinking is advisable. Care should be taken not to exploit the young, the immature or those who are mentally or socially vulnerable.

46.4 Advertisements should not be directed at people under eighteen through the selection of media, style of presentation, content or context in which they appear. No medium should be used to advertise alcoholic drinks if more than 25% of its audience is under eighteen years of age.

46.5 People shown drinking should not be, nor should they look, under twenty-five. Younger models may be shown in advertisements, for example in the context of family celebrations, but it should be obvious that they are not drinking.

46.6 Advertisements should not feature real or fictitious characters who are likely to appeal particularly to people under eighteen in a way that would encourage them to drink.

46.7 Advertisements should not suggest that any alcoholic drink can enhance mental, physical or sexual capabilities, popularity, attractiveness, masculinity, femininity or sporting achievements.

46.8 Advertisements may give factual information about the alcoholic strength of a drink or its relatively high alcohol content but this should not be the dominant theme of any advertisement. Alcoholic drinks should not be presented as preferable because of their high alcohol content or intoxicating effect.

46.9 Advertisements should not portray drinking alcohol as the main reason for the success of any personal relationship or social event. A brand preference may be promoted as a mark of the drinker's good taste and discernment.

46.10 Drinking alcohol should not be portrayed as a challenge, nor should it be suggested that people who drink are brave, tough or daring for doing so.

46.11 Particular care should be taken to ensure that advertisements for sales promotions requiring multiple purchases do not actively encourage excessive consumption.

46.12 Advertisements should not depict activities or locations where drinking alcohol would be unsafe or unwise. In particular, advertisements should not associate the consumption of alcohol with operating machinery, driving, any activity relating to water or heights, or any other occupation that requires concentration in order to be done safely.

46.13 Low alcohol drinks are those that contain 1.2% alcohol by volume or less. Advertisers should ensure that low alcohol drinks are not promoted in a way that encourages their inappropriate consumption and should not depict activities that require complete sobriety.

Children

47.1 The way in which children perceive and react to advertisements is influenced by their age, experience and the context in which the message is delivered. The ASA will take these factors into account when assessing advertisements.

47.2 Advertisements and promotions addressed to or featuring children should contain nothing that is likely to result in their physical, mental or moral harm:

a   they should not be encouraged to enter strange places or talk to strangers. Care is needed when they are asked to make collections, enter schemes or gather labels, wrappers, coupons and the like

b   they should not be shown in hazardous situations or behaving dangerously in the home or outside except to promote safety. Children should not be shown unattended in street scenes unless they are old enough to take responsibility for their own safety. Pedestrians and cyclists should be seen to observe the Highway Code

c   they should not be shown using or in close proximity to dangerous substances or equipment without direct adult supervision. Examples include matches, petrol, certain medicines and household substances as well as certain electrical appliances and machinery, including agricultural equipment

d   they should not be encouraged to copy any practice that might be unsafe for a child.

47.3   Advertisements and promotions addressed to or featuring children should not exploit their credulity, loyalty, vulnerability or lack of experience:

a   they should not be made to feel inferior or unpopular for not buying the advertised product

b   they should not be made to feel that they are lacking in courage, duty or loyalty if they do not buy or do not encourage others to buy a particular product

c   it should be made easy for them to judge the size, characteristics and performance of any product advertised and to distinguish between real-life situations and fantasy

d   parental permission should be obtained before they are committed to purchasing complex and costly goods and services.

47.4 Advertisements and promotions addressed to children:

a should not actively encourage them to make a nuisance of themselves to parents or others

b should not make a direct appeal to purchase unless the product is one that would be likely to interest children and that they could reasonably afford. Mail order advertisers should take care when using youth media not to promote products that are unsuitable for children

c should not exaggerate what is attainable by an ordinary child using the product being advertised or promoted

d should not actively encourage them to eat or drink at or near bedtime, to eat frequently throughout the day or to replace main meals with confectionery or snack foods

e should not exploit their susceptibility to charitable appeals and should explain the extent to which their participation will help in any charity-linked promotions.

47.5 Promotions addressed to children:

a should not encourage excessive purchases in order to participate

b should make clear that parental permission is required if prizes and incentives might cause conflict between children and their parents. Examples include animals, bicycles, tickets for outings, concerts and holidays

c should clearly explain the number and type of any additional proofs of purchase needed to participate

d should contain a prominent closing date

e should not exaggerate the value of prizes or the chances of winning them.

Motoring

48.1 Advertisements for motor vehicles, fuel or accessories should avoid portraying or referring to practices that encourage anti-social behaviour.

48.2 Advertisers should not make speed or acceleration claims the predominant message of their advertisements. However it is legitimate to give general information about a vehicle's performance such as acceleration statistics, braking power, roadholding and top and mid-range speeds.

48.3 Advertisers should not portray speed in a way that might encourage motorists to drive irresponsibly or to break the law.

48.4 Vehicles should not be depicted in dangerous or unwise situations in a way that would encourage irresponsible driving. Their capabilities may be demonstrated on a track or circuit provided it is clearly not in use as a public highway.

48.5 Care should be taken in cinema advertisements and those in electronic media where the moving image may give the impression of exceptional speed. In all cases where vehicles are shown in normal driving circumstances on the public road they should be seen not to exceed UK speed limits.

48.6 When making environmental claims for their products, advertisers should conform with the Specific Rules on Environmental Claims.

48.7 Prices quoted should correspond to the vehicles illustrated. For example, it is not acceptable to feature only a top-of-the-range model alongside the starting price for that range.

48.8 Safety claims should not exaggerate the benefit to consumers. Advertisers should not make absolute claims about safety unless they hold evidence to support them.

Environmental claims

49.1 The basis of any claim should be explained clearly and should be qualified where necessary. Unqualified claims can mislead if they omit significant information.

49.2 Claims such as 'environmentally friendly' or 'wholly biodegradable' should not be used without qualification unless advertisers can provide convincing evidence that their product will cause no environmental damage. Qualified claims and comparisons such as 'greener' or 'friendlier' may be acceptable if advertisers can substantiate that their product provides an overall improvement in environmental terms either against their competitors' or their own previous products.

49.3 Where there is a significant division of scientific opinion or where evidence is inconclusive this should be reflected in any statements made in the advertisement. Advertisers should not suggest that their claims command universal acceptance if it is not the case.

49.4 If a product has never had a demonstrably adverse effect on the environment, advertisements should not imply that the formulation has changed to make it safe. It is legitimate, however, to make claims about a product whose composition has changed or has always been designed in a way that omits chemicals known to cause damage to the environment.

49.5 The use of extravagant language should be avoided, as should bogus and confusing scientific terms. If it is necessary to use a scientific expression, its meaning should be clear.

Health and beauty products and therapies

General

50.1 Medical and scientific claims made about beauty and health-related products should be backed by trials, where appropriate conducted on people. Substantiation will be assessed by the ASA on the basis of established scientific knowledge.

50.2 Advertisers should not discourage people from having essential treatment; medical advice is needed for serious or prolonged ailments and advertisers should not offer medicines or therapies for them.

50.3 Advice, diagnosis or treatment of any serious medical condition should be conducted face-to-face. Advertisers inviting consumers to diagnose their own minor ailments should not make claims that might lead to a mistaken diagnosis.

50.4 Consumers should not be encouraged to use products to excess and advertisers should not suggest that their products or therapies are guaranteed to work, absolutely safe or without side-effects for everyone.

50.5 Advertisements should not suggest that any product is safe or effective merely because it is 'natural' or that it is generally safer because it omits an ingredient in common use.

50.6 Advertisers offering individual treatments, particularly those that are physically invasive, may be asked by the media and the ASA to provide full details together with information about those who will supervise and administer them. Where appropriate, practitioners should have relevant and recognised qualifications. Consumers should be encouraged to take independent medical advice before committing themselves to significant treatments.

50.7 References to the relief of symptoms or the superficial signs of ageing are acceptable if they can be substantiated. Unqualified claims such as 'cure' and 'rejuvenation' are not generally acceptable.

50.8 Claims made for the treatment of minor addictions and bad habits should make clear the vital role of willpower.

50.9 Advertisers should not use unfamiliar scientific words for common conditions.

Medicines

50.10 The Medicines Act 1968 and its regulations, as well as regulations implementing European Community Directive 92/28/EEC, govern the advertising and promotion of medicines and the conditions of ill health that they can be offered to treat. Guidance on the legislation is available from the Medicines Control Agency (MCA).

50.11 Medicines must be licensed by the MCA before they are advertised and any claims made for products must conform with the licence. Unlicensed products should not make medicinal claims. Advertisements should refer to the MCA, the licence or the EC only if required to do so by the MCA.

50.12 Prescription-only medicines may not be advertised to the public. Health-related claims in advertisements and promotions addressed only to the medical and allied professions are exempt from the Codes.

50.13 Advertisements should include the name of the product, an indication of what it is for, text such as 'Always read the label' and the common name of the active ingredient if there is only one. There should be no suggestion that any medicine is either a food or a cosmetic.

50.14 Advertisers must not use fear or anxiety to promote medicines or recovery from illness and should not suggest that using or avoiding a product can affect normal good health.

50.15 Illustrations of the effect or action of any product on the human body should be accurate.

50.16 Advertisements for medicines should not be addressed to children.

50.17 Advertisers should not use health professionals or celebrities to endorse medicines.

50.18 Advertisements for any medicine should not claim that its effects are as good as or better than those of another identifiable product.

50.19 Homeopathic medicinal products must be registered in the UK. Any product information given in the advertisement should be confined to what appears on the label. Advertisements should include a warning to consult a doctor if symptoms persist and should not make any medicinal or therapeutic claims or refer to any ailment.

Vitamins, minerals and food supplements

50.20 Advertisers should hold scientific evidence for any claim that their vitamin or mineral product or food supplement is beneficial to health.

50.21 A well-balanced diet should provide the vitamins and minerals needed each day by a normal, healthy individual. Advertisers may offer supplements as a safeguard, but should not suggest that there is widespread vitamin or mineral deficiency or that it is necessary or therapeutic to augment a well-balanced diet. Advertisements should not imply that supplements will guard against deficiency, elevate mood or enhance performance. Supplements should not be promoted as a substitute for a healthy diet.

50.22 Certain groups of people may benefit from vitamin and mineral supplementation. These include people who eat nutritionally inadequate meals, the elderly, children and adolescents, convalescents, athletes in training, those who are physically very active, women of child-bearing age, lactating and pregnant women and dieters. In assessing claims the ASA will bear in mind recommendations made by the Department of Health.

50.23 Serious vitamin and mineral depletion caused by illness should be diagnosed and treated by a doctor. Self-medication should not be promoted on the basis that it will influence the speed or extent of recovery.

Cosmetics

50.24 Claims made about the action that a cosmetic has on or in the skin should distinguish between the composition of the product and any effects brought about by the way in which it is applied, such as massage. Scientific evidence should also make this distinction.

50.25 Some cosmetics have an effect on the kind of skin changes that are caused by environmental factors. Advertisements for them can therefore refer to temporarily preventing, delaying or masking premature ageing.

Hair and scalp

50.26 Advertisers should be able to provide scientific evidence, where appropriate in the form of trials conducted on people, for any claim that their product or therapy can prevent baldness or slow it down, arrest or reverse hair loss, stimulate or improve hair growth, nourish hair roots, strengthen the hair or improve its health as distinct from its appearance.

Slimming

51.1 A slimming regime in which the intake of energy is lower than its output is the main self-treatment for achieving weight loss. Any claims made for the effectiveness or action of a slimming method or product should be backed where appropriate by rigorous practical trials on people; testimonials that are not supported by trials do not constitute substantiation.

51.2 Advertisements for any slimming regime or establishment should neither be directed at, nor contain anything that will appeal particularly to, people who are under eighteen.

51.3 Obesity is a condition in which the subject's weight is more than 20% above the ideal range for their height or whose Body Mass Index is more than 30. Obesity requires medical attention and treatments for it should not be advertised to the public unless they are to be used under qualified supervision.

51.4 Advertisements should not suggest that it is desirable to be underweight.

51.5 Before claims are made that weight or inch loss can be achieved by expelling water, speeding up the metabolism, using mechanical devices, wearing garments or applying substances to the skin they must be substantiated with scientific evidence of the method's effect on people. Combining a diet with an unproven weight loss method does not justify making slimming claims for the method.

51.6 Advertisers should be able to show that their diet plans are nutritionally well-balanced. This will be assessed in relation to the kind of subjects who would be using them.

51.7 Vitamins and minerals do not contribute to weight loss, but may be offered to slimmers as a safeguard against any shortfall when dieting.

51.8 Crash diets are those that fall below 400 Calories a day. They should not be advertised to dieters unless they are to be used under direct medical supervision.

51.9 Diet aids such as low-calorie foods, food substitutes, appetite depressants and meal replacements should make clear how they work. They should state that they cannot aid slimming except as part of a diet in which the total calorie intake is controlled. Prominence must be given to the role of the diet, and advertisements should not give the impression that dieters cannot fail or can eat as much as they like and still lose weight.

51.10 Advertisements should not contain general claims that precise amounts of weight can be lost within a stated period or that weight can be lost from specific parts of the body. Claims that individuals have lost exact amounts of weight should be compatible with good medical and nutritional practice, should give details of the time period involved and should not be based on unrepresentative experiences.

51.11 Both physical and passive exercise improve muscle tone slowly and this can have an effect on body shape. An improvement in posture may also benefit the figure. Advertisers should be able to substantiate any claims that such methods used alone or in conjunction with a diet plan can lead to weight or inch loss. Advertisements for intensive exercise programmes should encourage users to check with a doctor before starting.

51.12 Short-term loss of girth may be achieved by wearing a tight-fitting garment. This should not be portrayed as permanent, nor should it be confused with weight loss.

Distance selling

52.1 Distance selling involves offering goods or services to consumers without the buyer and seller at any time meeting face-to-face. Advertisers, promoters and all others involved in handling responses must observe the Codes.

52.2 Advertisements should state the full name and address of the advertisers outside the coupon or other response mechanism so that it can be retained by consumers. A separate address for orders may also be given; this need not be a full address but could, for example, be a Freepost address or PO Box number.

52.3 Unless obvious from the context, advertisements should include:

a the main characteristics of the product or service

b the amount and number of any transport charges

c any VAT payable, unless the advertisement is addressed exclusively to the trade

d a statement that goods can be returned, if applicable

e any limitation on the offer and any conditions that affect its validity

f the estimated delivery time; consumers should be advised if orders cannot be fulfilled within thirty days. Those who have paid in advance should be offered a refund but if they prefer to wait they should be given a firm despatch date or fortnightly progress reports.

52.4 Advertisers should take no longer than thirty days to fulfil orders except:

a where security is provided for purchasers' money through an independent scheme

b for goods such as plants and made-to-measure products where the estimated time of delivery should be made clear c where the advertisers make clear that they do not intend to begin production unless a sufficient response is received

d where a series of goods is sent at regular intervals after the first thirty days.

52.5 Before goods or services are supplied and accepted advertisers should, where appropriate, provide consumers with written information on:

a payment arrangements, including credit and instalment terms

b how to exercise their right to withdraw

c the cancellation of open-ended contracts

d other terms and conditions, including guarantees

e the most appropriate address to contact them.

52.6 Advertisers must refund money promptly when:

a consumers have not received their goods or services; alternatively advertisers may, if asked, provide a replacement

b goods are returned because they are damaged when received, are faulty or are not as described, in which case the advertisers must bear the cost of transit in both directions

c unwanted goods are returned undamaged within seven working days of being received by the purchaser; consumers should assume they can try out goods unless the advertisement states otherwise. It should be made clear if consumers have to pay the return postage

d an unconditional money-back guarantee is given and the goods are returned within a reasonable period

e goods that have been returned are not received back, provided consumers can produce proof of posting.

52.7 Advertisers do not have to provide a full refund on:

a perishable, personalised or made-to-measure goods so long as all contractual obligations to consumers are met

b high value products, or those to be delivered abroad, where an administration fee may be charged; this should be made clear to consumers before they are committed

c goods that can be copied unless they fall under 52.6*a*, *b* or *c*.

52.8 If advertisers intend to call on respondents personally this should be made clear in the advertisement or in a follow-up mailing. To allow consumers an adequate opportunity to refuse a personal visit, advertisers should provide a reply-paid postcard or Freephone telephone contact instructions.

52.9 Advertisers should take particular care when packaging products that may fall into the hands of children.

List and database practice

53.1 List owners, brokers and users should:

a ensure that their lists are run against the most recent quarterly Mailing Preference Service (MPS) Suppression File and are accurate and up-to-date

b be able to identify anyone who has objected in the last five years, or who has not had an opportunity to object, to their inclusion on any list that is to be disclosed to others

c avoid duplication

d act promptly to correct personal information

e ensure that anyone who has been notified as dead is not mailed again and, where appropriate, should refer the notifier to the MPS

f comply with the provisions of the Data Protection Act 1984.

53.2 List users should:

a   ensure, where possible, that those approached are not inappropriate for the offer

b   not use lists or selections from lists that are more than six months old unless they have been updated

c   inform the list owner of any requested corrections within sixty days

d   if asked, give the sources of names on their list promptly to anyone listed or to the ASA.

53.3 List owners should:

a   satisfy themselves, and obtain an assurance from list users, that any literature used in an offer complies with the Codes

b   make corrections or suppressions themselves, or ensure that list users do, if a mailing is delayed by more than six months

c   require list users to inform them of requests for correction within sixty days

d   be able to demonstrate their compliance with this Code regarding list rental.

53.4 Where it is not obvious from the context, consumers should be informed by anyone asking for personal information:

a   why it is being collected

b   who is collecting it

c   the reason for collecting extensive information and, if it is intended to disclose it to others, their names

d   whether it is intended to make the information available to others, including associated companies; before information is disclosed to any other company for the first time, consumers should be given an opportunity to object.

53.5 If, after collection, it is decided to use information for a purpose that is significantly different from the one originally intended, consumers must be advised and given thirty days to object.

53.6 The extent and detail of personal information held for any purpose should be adequate, relevant and should not be excessive for that purpose.

53.7 Personal information must always be held securely and should be safeguarded against unauthorised use, disclosure, alteration or destruction.

53.8 Individuals are entitled to have their names removed from any mailing list. However, if they want to reduce all their mailings significantly, they should be referred to the MPS.

53.9 Individuals who have asked for information about them to be suppressed should not be contacted again for a minimum of five years from the date of their request unless they ask to be reinstated.

53.10 Businesses are permitted to use any published information that is generally available provided the individual concerned is not listed on the MPS Suppression File.

Employment and business opportunities

54.1 Advertisers should distinguish clearly between offers of employment and business opportunities. Before publication, media normally require full details of the advertisers and any terms and conditions imposed on respondents.

54.2 Employment advertisements must correspond to genuine vacancies and potential employees must not be asked to send money for further details. Living and working conditions should not be misrepresented. Quoted earnings should be precise; if a forecast has to be made this should not be unrepresentative. If income is earned from a basic salary and commission, commission only, or in some other way, this should be made clear.

54.3 An employment agency must make clear in advertisements that it is an employment agency.

54.4 Homework schemes require participants to make articles, perform services or offer facilities at or from home. Consumers should be given:

a   the full name and address of the advertisers

b   a clear description of the work; the support available to homeworkers should not be exaggerated

c   an indication of whether participants are self-employed or employed by a business

d   the likely level of earnings, but only if this can be supported with evidence of the experience of current homeworkers

e   no forecast of earnings if the scheme is new

f   details of any required investment or binding obligation

g   details of any charges for raw materials, machines, components, administration and the like

h   information on whether the advertisers will buy back any goods made

i   any limitations or conditions that might influence consumers prior to their decision to participate.

54.5 Advertisements for business opportunities should contain:

a   the name and contact details of the advertisers

b   where possible, a clear description of the work involved and the extent of investors' commitments, including any financial investment; the support available should not be exaggerated

c   no unrepresentative or exaggerated earnings figures.

54.6 Vocational training and other instruction courses should make no promises of employment unless it is guaranteed. The duration of the course and the level of attainment needed to embark on it should be made clear.

54.7 The sale of directories giving details of employment or business opportunities should indicate plainly the nature of what is being offered.

Financial services and products

55.1 The rules that follow provide only general guidance. Advertisers, their agencies and the media must also comply with the numerous statutes that govern financial services and products including issuing advertisements, investment opportunities, credit facilities and the provision of financial information.

55.2 Offers of financial services and products should be set out in a way that allows them to be understood easily by the audience being addressed. Advertisers should ensure that they do not take advantage of people's inexperience or gullibility.

55.3 Advertisers asking for a commitment at a distance should make sure that their full address is given outside any response coupon or other mechanism.

55.4 Advertisements should indicate the nature of the contract being offered, any limitations, expenses, penalties and charges and the terms of withdrawal. Alternatively, where an advertisement is short or general in its content, free explanatory material giving full details of the offer should be readily available before a binding contract is entered into.

55.5 The basis used to calculate any rates of interest, forecasts or projections should be apparent immediately.

55.6 Advertisements should make clear that the value of investments is variable and, unless guaranteed, can go down as well as up. If the value of the investment is guaranteed details should be included in the advertisement.

55.7 Advertisements should specify that past performance or experience does not necessarily give a guide for the future. Any examples used should not be unrepresentative.

Cigarette Code

Introduction

66.1 The Cigarette Code is exceptional in that it is the outcome of discussions between the UK Departments of Health (DH), the manufacturers and importers of cigarettes (represented by the Tobacco Manufacturers Association and the Imported Tobacco Products Advisory Council respectively) and the Advertising Standards Authority (ASA). It runs in parallel with, and its rules are applied in addition to, those imposed elsewhere in the British Codes of Advertising and Sales Promotion.

66.2 The ASA is the final arbiter of the meaning of the Cigarette Code's rules. The ASA deals with complaints about advertisement content and also supervises the advisory and the mandatory pre-clearance procedure for cigarette advertisements operated by the Committee of Advertising Practice (CAP).

66.3 The Cigarette Code governs the content of advertisements. It is one part of a wider voluntary agreement between the DH and the tobacco industry. This agreement also covers advertising expenditure, media selection, health warnings and promotions. There is a separate agreement on sports sponsorship between the Department of National Heritage, on behalf of HM Government, and the tobacco industry. This includes a provision encouraging advertisers of sponsored sporting events to follow the Cigarette Code. Complaints relating to breaches of these two agreements should be addressed to the Committee for Monitoring Agreements on Tobacco Advertising and Sponsorship (COMATAS).

66.4 The rules are not intended to hamper fair competition. Advertisers of cigarettes and hand-rolling tobacco are free to attract attention to their products, provided both the spirit and the letter of the Codes are observed.

Scope

66.5 The Cigarette Code applies to advertisements for:

a   cigarettes and their components such as tobacco and tobacco substitutes

b   hand-rolling tobacco

c   cigarette papers, filters and wrappings

d   any product if the advertisement concerned features a cigarette or pack design of a recognisable brand available in the UK

e   teasers

f   special offers, competitions and other sales promotions

g   products displaying the colours, livery, insignia or name of a cigarette brand in a way that promotes smoking rather than these other branded products.

66.6 The Cigarette Code does not apply to advertisements for:

a   cigars, cheroots, cigarillos, pipe tobacco or snuff

b   herbal cigarettes and tobaccos

c   cigarette holders, matches, lighters and the like except when covered by 66.5 above

d   schemes, events or activities sponsored or supported financially by manufacturers of products listed in 66.5 above, even where such advertisements are for sports sponsorship and are required by the voluntary agreement on sports sponsorship to carry a health warning

e   advertisements and promotions addressed to the trade in media not targeted at the public.

General principles and procedures

66.7 The rules which follow in clauses 66.13–66.26 should be observed in the spirit as well as in the letter.

66.8 Claims encompass statements and visual presentations and can be direct or indirect. Claims which the ASA or CAP regard as eroding or diminishing the effectiveness of the rules will be judged contrary to the spirit of the Code; humour is acceptable provided it is used with care and is not likely to have a particular appeal to the young.

66.9 Advertisements for cigarettes or hand-rolling tobacco should have a signed, dated and numbered certificate of clearance from CAP before being displayed or published.

66.10 Certificates will be valid for advertisements in current campaigns after which time the copy must be re-certified. Clearance can be universal or may be media-specific in that certain advertisements might only be acceptable for publication in a limited circulation medium. Certificates will be endorsed accordingly.

66.11 Point of sale material featuring themes or elements already cleared in general media advertisements should normally need no additional clearance from CAP. However, the acceptability of extracted themes or elements will depend on the context and spirit in which they are used. These must not differ from the original advertisements. Whenever new treatments or developments of existing themes are introduced they should be checked with CAP to ascertain whether a certificate is needed.

66.12 CAP clearance does not automatically protect advertisements against complaints to the ASA Council which acts as the final arbiter of the meaning of the Code's rules.

Rules

66.13 No advertisement should incite people to start smoking.

66.14 Advertisements should not encourage smokers to increase their consumption or smoke to excess. Smokers should not be encouraged to buy or stock large quantities of cigarettes.

66.15 Advertisements for coupon brands should not feature products unless these can be obtained through the redemption of coupons collected over a reasonable period of average consumption.

66.16 Advertisements should never suggest that smoking is safe, healthy, natural, necessary for relaxation and concentration, popular or appropriate in all circumstances. Cigarettes should not be shown in the mouth and advertisements should not associate smoking with healthy eating or drinking.

66.17 No more than half of those shown in groups should be smoking; smoking should not be shown in public places where it is usually not permitted.

66.18 People can be shown smoking while engaged in work or leisure activities provided that the advertisement does not illustrate inappropriate smoking situations.

66.19 Smoking should not be associated with social, sexual, romantic or business success and advertisements should not be sexually titillating, though the choice of a particular brand may be linked to taste and discernment. In particular, advertisements should not link smoking with people who are evidently wealthy, fashionable, sophisticated or successful or who possess other attributes or qualities that may reasonably be expected to command admiration or encourage emulation.

66.20 Advertisements should not contain actual or implied testimonials or endorsements from well-known people, famous fictitious characters or people doing jobs or occupying positions which are generally regarded as admirable.

66.21 No heroic figure, personality cult, pastime or fashion trend should be featured in advertisements in a way that would appeal to those who are adventurous or rebellious, particularly the young.

66.22 No advertisement should play on the susceptibilities of those who are physically or emotionally vulnerable, particularly the young or immature. Advertisements should therefore avoid employing any approach which is more likely to attract the attention or sympathy of those under the age of eighteen.

66.23 Anyone shown smoking should always be, and clearly be seen to be, over twenty-five.

66.24 No advertisement should exaggerate the pleasure of smoking or claim that it is daring or glamorous to smoke or that smoking enhances people's masculinity, femininity, appearance or independence.

66.25 Advertisements that employ outdoor locations or those that depict people or animals should avoid any suggestion of a healthy or wholesome style of life. Any locations, people and objects depicted should not have undue aspirational, historical or cultural associations.

66.26 Advertisements should not associate smoking with sport or with active or outdoor games. Advertisements for sports sponsorship are governed by a separate voluntary agreement with the Department of National Heritage, on behalf of HM Government, and the tobacco industry.

Legislation

67 The following list of statutes and regulations affecting advertising and promotions relates to England and Wales and is not exhaustive. Many of these statutes are also applicable to Scotland and Northern Ireland which have their own additional legislation. Businesses have primary responsibility for ensuring that everything they do is legal.

The general law on matters such as contract, negligence, libel and intellectual property should also be observed.

Accommodation Agencies Act 1953
Administration of Justice Act 1985
Adoption Act 1976
Alcoholic Liquor Duties Act 1979
Architects Registration Act 1938
Banking Act 1987
Betting and Gaming Duties Act 1981
Betting Gaming and Lotteries Acts 1963-1985
Bingo Act 1992
British Telecommunications Act 1981
Broadcasting Act 1990
Building Societies Act 1986
Business Advertisements (Disclosure) Order 1977
Business Names Act 1985
Cancer Act 1939
Charities Act 1992 and Regulations
Children and Young Persons (Harmful Publications) Act 1955

Legislation

Children and Young Persons Acts 1933 and 1963
Civil Aviation Act 1982
Civil Aviation (Air Travel Organisers Licensing) Regulations 1972
Companies Act 1985
Competition Act 1980
Conduct of Employment Agencies and Employment Businesses Regulations 1976
Consumer Credit Act 1974
Consumer Credit (Advertisements) Regulations 1989
Consumer Credit (Exempt Advertisements) Order 1985
Consumer Protection Act 1987 and the Code of Practice for Traders on Price Indications
Consumer Safety Act 1978
Consumer Transactions (Restrictions on Statements) Order 1976
Control of Misleading Advertisements Regulations 1988
Copyright Designs and Patents Act 1988
Cream Regulations 1970
Credit Unions Act 1979
Crossbows Act 1987
Customs and Excise Management Act 1979
Data Protection Act 1984
Defamation Act 1952
Dentists Act 1984
Education Act 1944
Education (Schools) Act 1992
Employment Agencies Act 1973
Endangered Species (Import and Export) Act 1976/EC Directives 1979 and 1983 and Regulations 1983
Energy Act 1976
Estate Agents Act 1979
European Communities Act 1972
Fair Trading Act 1973
Finance Act 1981
Financial Services Act 1986 and Investment Advertisement Exemption Orders
Firearms Act 1968
Firearms (Dangerous Air Weapons) Rules 1969
Food Labelling Regulations 1984
Food Safety Act 1990 and Regulations
Forgery and Counterfeiting Act 1981
Foster Children Act 1980
Friendly Societies Acts 1986 and 1992

Gaming Act 1968
General Optical Council (Rules and Publicity) Order of Council 1985
Geneva Conventions Act 1957
Hallmarking Act 1973
Health Services and Public Health Act 1968
Hearing Aid Council Act 1968
Hearing Aid Council (Amendment) Act 1989
Income and Corporation Taxes Act 1988
Industrial and Provident Societies Act 1965
Insurance Brokers (Registration) Act 1977
Insurance Brokers Registration Council (Code of Conduct) Approval Order 1978
Insurance Companies Act 1982
Insurance Companies Regulations 1981
Insurance Companies (Advertisements) (Amendments) No 2 Regulations 1983
Licensing Act 1964
Local Government Act 1992
Local Government (Miscellaneous Provisions) Act 1982
London Cab Acts 1968 and 1973
Lotteries and Amusements Act 1976 and Amendments
Mail Order Transactions (Information) Order 1976
Malicious Communications Act 1988
Margarine Regulations 1967
Marine etc Broadcasting (Offences) Act 1967
Medicines Act 1968
Medicines (Advertising) Regulations 1994
Medicines (Exemptions from Restrictions on the Retail Sale or Supply of Veterinary Drugs) Order 1979
Medicines (Monitoring of Advertising) Regulations 1994
Milk and Milk Products (Protection of Designations) Regulations 1990
Misrepresentation Act 1976
Mock Auctions Act 1961
National Lottery etc Act 1993 and National Lottery Regulations 1994
Nightwear (Safety) Regulations 1985
Nurseries and Child Minders Regulation Act 1948
Nurses Agencies Act 1957
Nurses Midwives and Health Visitors Act 1979

Obscene Publications Act 1959
Opticians Act 1989 and Regulations
Package Travel, Package Holidays and Package Tours Regulations 1992
Passenger Car Fuel Consumption Order 1983
Prevention of Corruption Acts 1889-1916
Price Indications (Method of Payment) Regulations 1991
Price Marking Order 1991
Price Marking (Amendment) Order 1994
Professions Supplementary to Medicine Act 1960
Property Misdescriptions Act 1991
Protection of Children (Tobacco) Act 1986
Pyramid Selling Schemes Regulations 1989
Pyramid Selling Schemes (Amendment) Regulations 1990
Race Relations Act 1976
Registered Designs Act 1949
Registered Homes Act 1984
Rent Act 1977
Representation of the People Act 1983
Restriction of Offensive Weapons Act 1959
Restriction on Agreements (Estate Agents) Order 1970
Restrictive Trade Practices Acts 1976 and 1977
Road Traffic Act 1988
Road Traffic (Driving Instruction) Act 1984
Sale of Goods Act 1979
Sex Discrimination Acts 1975 and 1986
Shops Act 1950
Shops (Early Closing Days) Act 1965
Social Security Act 1986
Solicitors Act 1974
Sunday Entertainments Act 1932
Sunday Observance Act 1780
Sunday Trading Act 1994
Sunday Theatre Act 1972
Supply of Goods and Services Act 1982
Surrogacy Arrangements Act 1985
Tattooing of Minors Act 1969
Telecommunications Act 1984
Telecommunications Apparatus (Advertisements) Order 1985
Telecommunications Apparatus (Marketing & Labelling) Order 1985
Textile Products (Indications of Fibre Content) Regulations 1986
Theft Acts 1968 and 1978
Timeshare Act 1992
Torts (Interference with Goods) Act 1977
Trade Descriptions Act 1968
Trade Descriptions (Sealskin Goods) (Information) Order 1980
Trade Marks Act 1994
Trading Stamps Act 1964
Unfair Contract Terms Act 1977
Unsolicited Goods and Services Acts 1971 and 1975
Unsolicited Goods and Services (Amendment) Act 1975
Vagrancy Act 1824
Venereal Diseases Act 1917
Veterinary Surgeons Act 1966
Weights and Measures Act 1985
Wildlife and Countryside Act 1981
Wireless Telegraphy Act 1949

How the system works

The self-regulatory system

68.1 The self-regulatory system includes advertisers and promoters, their agencies, the media and the trade and professional organisations of the advertising and sales promotion businesses. Through the Committee of Advertising Practice (CAP) their task is to ensure that advertisements and sales promotions that are commissioned, prepared, placed or published in the UK conform to the rules in the British Codes of Advertising and Sales Promotion drawn up by CAP.

68.2 The strength of the system depends on the long-term commitment of all those involved in commercial communications. Practitioners in every sphere share an interest in seeing that advertisements and promotions are welcomed and trusted by their audience; unless they are accepted and believed they cannot succeed. If they are offensive or misleading they discredit everyone associated with them and the industry as a whole.

68.3 The UK's self-regulatory system is recognised by the Government and has been examined by the judiciary; it provides an effective complement to UK and EC law.

68.4 The roles of CAP, the Advertising Standards Authority (ASA) and their joint Secretariat which is responsible for the day to day work of both organisations are described below.

The Committee of Advertising Practice

68.5 CAP co-ordinates the activities of its members to achieve the highest degree of compliance with the Codes. CAP devises, reviews and amends the Codes, administers the mandatory pre-clearance of cigarette advertising, gives free and confidential pre-publication advice to advertisers and promoters, their agencies, the media and others, produces Advice Notes and Ad Alerts for the industry and co-ordinates the sanctions operated by its members. Favourable pre-publication advice does not automatically protect advertisers or promoters from complaints being investigated by the ASA.

68.6 The Codes establish a standard against which advertisements can be assessed. Additional codes exist in many other sectors; where appropriate these require practitioners to conform with the CAP Codes.

68.7 The Chairman of CAP is elected by its members and normally holds office for two years. The Chairman is succeeded by the Vice Chairman, who is elected in the same way; both usually come from businesses with advertising interests.

68.8 CAP actively encourages participation in the self-regulatory system. Suggestions for improving the Codes' rules or modifying their application should be sent in writing to the Chairman. If changes are adopted by CAP their introduction is normally deferred for a short time to give advertisers an adequate opportunity to amend their advertisements.

68.9 Much of the detailed work of CAP is done by its two standing Review Panels which meet regularly, or by one of its *ad hoc* Working Groups. The General Media Review Panel concentrates on all advertising, media and issues other than those relating to sales promotions, direct marketing and mail order. The Sales Promotion and Direct Response Review Panel, as its name suggests, is responsible for these sectors. Each Review Panel is composed of industry experts together with one ASA Council member. The Panels guide the Secretariat and help the ASA and CAP to produce advice for the industry and to interpret the Codes both in individual cases and on broad issues. In addition, the Panels provide a forum to review recommendations and advice given by the Secretariat.

68.10 Working Groups are convened for limited periods to address specific issues arising out of the self-regulatory process.

The Advertising Standards Authority

68.11 The ASA was established in 1962 to provide independent scrutiny of the newly created self-regulatory system set up by the industry. Its chief tasks are to promote and enforce high standards in advertisements, to investigate complaints, to identify and resolve problems through its own research, to ensure that the system operates in the public interest and to act as the channel for communications with those who have an interest in advertising standards.

68.12 The ASA is a limited company, and is independent of both the Government and the advertising business. At least half of the twelve member Council appointed by the Chairman to govern the ASA is unconnected with the advertising business. Council members sit as individuals and are selected, as far as possible, to reflect a diversity of background and experience.

68.13 The ASA investigates complaints from any source against advertisements and promotions in non-broadcast media.

Companies are told the outcome of the ASA Council's rulings and, where appropriate, are asked to withdraw or amend their advertisements or promotions. The adjudications reached by the Council at its monthly meetings, as well as editorial guidance on current topics, are published in the ASA's Monthly Report. This is distributed free of charge to the media, libraries, government departments, politicians, businesses, consumer bodies and the public.

68.14 The ASA gives equal emphasis to conducting a substantial research and monitoring programme by reviewing issues, advertisements and promotions that fall within its scope. Particular media and product categories are also selected for scrutiny. In this way the ASA can identify trends and prevent future problems.

68.15 Publicising the ASA's policies and actions is essential to sustaining wide acceptance of the system's integrity. A comprehensive programme of seminars and speeches, advertising, leaflets, briefing notes on a wide range of topics, a video targeted at consumers and educational establishments and articles written for professional journals, newspapers and magazines all augment the ASA's extensive media coverage.

The administration of the system

68.16 The ASA and CAP share a joint Secretariat whose duties are organised to recognise the distinct functions of the two bodies. The Secretariat carries out the day-to-day work of the system and acts as a channel of communication, ensuring that industry expertise, specialist advice and the decisions of the ASA Council are co-ordinated and disseminated. The ASA and CAP form an independent judgement on any matter reported to them after they have considered the Secretariat's recommendations.

68.17 Advertisers and promoters bear principal responsibility for the advertisements and promotions they produce and must be able to prove the truth of their claims to the ASA; they have a duty to make their claims fair and honest and to avoid causing offence. Advertising and sales promotion agencies have an obligation to create advertisements and promotions that are accurate, ethical and do not mislead or offend. Publishers and media owners recognise that they should disseminate only those advertisements that conform with the Codes. This responsibility extends to any other agent involved in producing, placing or publishing advertisements or promotions. They accept the rulings of the ASA Council as binding.

68.18 Claims that are judged by the ASA Council to be offensive, or that are not or cannot be verified, will be deemed to be contrary to the Codes. Everyone responsible for commissioning, preparing, placing and publishing an advertisement or promotion containing such claims will be asked to act promptly to amend or withdraw it.

The law

68.19 Since the first Codes were published the number of laws designed to protect consumers has greatly increased. There are directives emanating from the European Community as well as more than one hundred UK statutes, orders and regulations affecting advertising and promotions (see clause 67 above). The ASA maintains a rapport with those responsible for initiating or administering any laws that have a bearing on advertising or promotions. The system is reinforced by the legal backup provided for the work of the ASA by the Control of Misleading Advertisements Regulations 1988 (see clause 68.33 below).

68.20 The Codes, and the self-regulatory framework that exists to administer them, were designed and have been developed to work within and to complement these legal controls. They provide an alternative, and in some instances the only, means of resolving disputes about advertisements and promotions. They also stimulate the adoption of high standards of practice in areas such as taste and decency that are extremely difficult to judge in law but that fundamentally affect consumer confidence in advertising and promotions.

68.21 There are also some important spheres that are governed by legislation enforced by local authority trading standards and environmental health officers. These include product packaging (except for on-pack promotions), weights and measures, statements on displays at point of sale, and the safety of products.

68.22 Many government departments and agencies administer consumer protection legislation that ranges far wider and deeper than could be enforced through self-regulatory codes of practice. In some instances, advertisers who break the law risk criminal prosecution or civil action. The Codes require advertisers and promoters to ensure that all their advertisements and promotions are legal, but the ASA is not a law enforcement body. Any matter that principally concerns a legal dispute will normally need to be resolved through law enforcement agencies or the Courts.

Media prerogative

68.23 The fact that an advertisement or promotion conforms to the Codes does not guarantee that every publisher will accept it. Media owners can refuse space to advertisements that break the Codes and they are also under no obligation to publish every advertisement offered to them.

Funding

68.24 The whole system is funded by surcharges on advertising and direct marketing expenditure. This is collected by the Advertising Standards Board of Finance, a body that operates independently of the ASA and CAP. This arrangement helps to ensure that the independent judgement of those who administer the self-regulatory system is not compromised.

Complaints

68.25 Complaints are investigated free of charge. They must be in writing, and should be accompanied by a copy of the advertisement or a note of where and when it appeared.

68.26 The identities of individual members of the public who complain are neither published nor revealed by the ASA to advertisers without their express permission. Only the courts or officials acting within their legal powers can compel the ASA to disclose to them information received in confidence. The identities of groups and of industry complainants such as competitors are disclosed and they must agree to the publication of their identities before their complaints can be pursued.

68.27 Equal weight is given to the investigation of all complaints irrespective of their source. However, before approaching the ASA, industry complainants should wherever possible endeavour to resolve their differences between themselves or through any trade or professional organisations of which they are members.

68.28 Members of the public who complain may be asked to assure the ASA that they have no commercial or other interest in registering a complaint. If they do have an interest, this will be disclosed to the advertiser and may be included in the ASA's published report.

68.29 Complaints are normally not pursued if the point at issue is the subject of simultaneous legal action. In certain cases it may be more appropriate for an investigation to be undertaken by other consumer protection bodies. If so, the ASA will provide information or will try to redirect the complainant to the most appropriate qualified source of assistance.

68.30 Complaints about advertisements and promotions that obviously conflict with the Codes are given priority. Other complaints fall into four broad categories: those that concern matters outside the scope of the Codes; those where the complainant's interpretation of either the advertisement, the promotion or the Codes does not correspond with the ASA's; those that indicate the advertiser or promoter needs to make some minor modification; and those that make out a well-founded case for investigation. If the Council has previously ruled on the advertisement or promotion the complainant is notified of its judgement. A leaflet describing the full complaints procedure is available on request.

68.31 The Secretariat conducts a fact-finding investigation into those complaints that are pursued, where necessary taking advice from expert external consultants, and produces for the ASA Council a recommendation based on its findings. Recommendations made by the Secretariat can, at its request or the request of those affected, be reviewed by the appropriate Review Panel. The final decision on complaints rests with the Council. The Secretariat is authorised by the Council to ask advertisers or promoters to take interim action if it is necessary to avoid further harm, for example in the case of a misleading or offensive advertisement or promotion.

68.32 Appeals against ASA adjudications should be made in writing to the ASA's Chairman; they should be accompanied by new evidence or should demonstrate a substantial flaw in the conclusion reached by the ASA Council.

68.33 Members of the Secretariat are always ready to discuss complaints with those involved, but cannot divulge confidential information except to the ASA's external consultants who are under an obligation not to disclose it. The ASA's opinion of individual advertisements, promotions or issues arising under the Codes may be circulated to interested parties.

68.34 The Codes require advertisers and promoters to produce documentary evidence to substantiate their claims. No provision is made for oral hearings before the Council or the Secretariat.

Sanctions

68.35 A number of sanctions exist to counteract advertisements and promotions that conflict with the Codes: the media may deny access to space; adverse publicity may result from rulings published in the ASA's Monthly Report; trading sanctions may be imposed or recognition revoked by the advertiser's, promoter's or agency's professional association; and financial incentives provided by trade, professional or media organisations may be withdrawn.

68.36 The ASA is recognised as one of the effective channels that exist to control advertisements and promotions. Under the Control of Misleading Advertisements Regulations 1988, if a misleading advertisement or promotion continues to appear after the Council has ruled against it, the ASA can refer the matter to the Director General of Fair Trading who can seek an undertaking from anyone responsible for commissioning, preparing or disseminating it that it will be discontinued. If this is not given or is not honoured, the OFT can seek an injunction from the court to prevent its further appearance. Anyone who defaults can be found to be in contempt of court, and is liable to be penalised accordingly.

Europe

68.37 Most member states of the European Union, and many non-EU European countries, have self-regulatory processes that are broadly similar to the system in the UK. The ASA is a founder member of the European Advertising Standards Alliance, the organisation that draws together all these European interests. The Alliance is located in Brussels and meets regularly to co-ordinate the promotion of self-regulation at a European level. Among its wide range of operations, it acts as a focal point for cross-border complaints investigated by individual members; consumers need only complain to their own self-regulatory body, no matter where the advertisement or promotion originated. Additional information on the activities and objectives of the Alliance is available from the ASA.

APPENDIX 2

CODE OF PRACTICE FOR TRADERS ON PRICE INDICATIONS

Published by, and reproduced here with permission of, the Department of Trade and Industry.

NOVEMBER 1988

Contents

Introduction	171
Definitions	173
Part 1. Price Comparisons	174
1.1 Price comparisons generally	174
1.2 Comparisons with trader's own previous price	175
General	175
Food, drink and perishable goods	176
Mail order traders	176
Making a series of reductions	177
1.3 Introductory offers, 'after-sale' or 'after-promotion' prices	177
1.4 Comparisons with prices related to different circumstances	178
1.5 Comparisons with another trader's prices	179
1.6 Comparisons with 'Recommended Retail Price' or similar	180
1.7 Pre-printed prices	181
1.8 References to value or worth	181
1.9 Sales or special events	181
1.10 Free offers	182
Part 2. Actual Price to the Consumer	182
2.1 Indicating two different prices	182
2.2 Incomplete information and non-optional extras	182
Products available in limited numbers or range	183
Prices relating to differing forms of products	183
Postage, packing and delivery charges	183
Value Added Tax	183
Service, cover and minimum charges in hotels, restaurants and similar establishments	184
Holiday and travel prices	185
Ticket prices	186
Call-out charges	186
Credit facilities	186
Insurance	186

Part 3. Price indications which become misleading after
 they have been given 187
3.1 General 187
3.2 Newspaper and magazine advertisements 187
3.3 Mail order advertisements, catalogues and leaflets 188
3.4 Selling through agents 188
3.5 Changes in the rate of value added tax 189

Part 4. Sale of new homes 189

Introduction

The Consumer Protection Act

1. The Consumer Protection Act 1987 makes it a criminal offence to give consumers a misleading price indication about goods, services, accommodation (including the sale of new homes) or facilities. It applies however you give the price indication – whether in a TV or press advertisement, in a catalogue or leaflet, on notices, price tickets or shelf-edge marking in stores, or if you give it orally, for example on the telephone. The term 'price indication' includes price comparisons as well as indications of a single price.

2. This code of practice is approved under section 25 of the Act which gives the Secretary of State power to approve codes of practice to give practical guidance to traders. It is addressed to traders and sets out what is good practice to follow in giving price indications in a wide range of different circumstances, so as to avoid giving misleading price indications. But the Act does not require you to do as this code tells you. You may still give price indications which do not accord with this code, provided they are not misleading. 'Misleading' is defined in section 21 of the Act.

The definition covers indications about any conditions attached to a price, about what you expect to happen to a price in future and what you say in price comparisons, as well as indications about the actual price the consumer will have to pay. It also applies in the same way to any indications you give about the way in which a price will be calculated.

Price comparisons

3. If you want to make price comparisons, you should do so only if you can show that they are accurate and valid. Indications which give only the price of the product are unlikely to be misleading if they are accurate and cover the total charge you will make. Comparisons with prices which you can show have been or are being charged for the same or similar goods, services, accommodation or facilities and have applied for a reasonable period are also unlikely to be misleading. Guidance on these matters is contained in this code.

Enforcement

4. Enforcement of the Consumer Protection Act 1987 is the responsibility of officers of the local weights and measures authority (in Northern Ireland, the Department of Economic Development) – usually called Trading Standards Officers. If a Trading Standards Officer has reasonable grounds to suspect that you have given a misleading price indication, the Act gives the Officer power to require you to produce any records relating to your business and to seize and detain goods or records which the Officer has reasonable grounds for believing may be required as evidence in court proceedings.

5. It may only be practicable for Trading Standards Officers to obtain from you the information necessary to carry out their duties under the Act. In these circumstances the Officer may seek information and assistance about both the claim and the supporting evidence from you. Be prepared to cooperate with Trading Standards Officers and respond to reasonable requests for information and assistance. The Act makes it an offence to obstruct a Trading Standards Officer intentionally or to fail (without good cause) to give any assistance or information the Officer may reasonably require to carry out duties under the Act.

Court proceedings

6. If you are taken to court for giving a misleading price indication, the court can take into account whether or not you have followed the Code. If you have done as the Code advises, that will not be an absolute defence but it will tend to show that you have not committed an offence. Similarly if you have done something the Code advises against doing it may tend to show that the price indication was misleading. If you do something which is not covered by the Code, your price indication will need to be judged only against the terms of the general offence. The Act provides for a defence of due diligence, that is, that you have taken all reasonable steps to avoid committing the offence of giving a misleading price indication, but failure to follow the Code of Practice may make it difficult to show this.

Regulations

7. The Act also provides power to make regulations about price indications and you should ensure that your price indications comply with any such regulations. There are none at present.

Other legislation

8. This Code deals only with the requirements of Part III of the Consumer Protection Act 1987. In some sectors there will be other relevant legislation. For example, price indications about credit terms must comply with the Consumer Credit Act 1974 and the regulations made under it, as well as with the Consumer Protection Act 1987.

Definitions

In this Code:

Accommodation	includes hotel and other holiday accommodation and new homes for sale freehold or on a lease of over 21 years but does not include rented homes.
Consumer	means anyone who might want the goods, services, accommodation or facilities, other than for business use.
Price	means both the total amount the consumer will have to pay to get the goods, services, accommodation or facilities and any method which has been or will be used to calculate that amount.
Price comparison	means any indication given to consumers that the price at which something is offered to consumers is less than or equal to some other price.

Product	means goods, services, accommodation and facilities (but not credit facilities, except where otherwise specified).
Services and Facilities	means any services or facilities whatever (including credit, banking and insurance services, purchase or sale of foreign currency, supply of electricity, off-street car parking and caravan sites) *except* those provided by a person who is an authorised person or appointed representative under the Financial Services Act 1986 in the course of an investment business, services provided by an employee to his employer and facilities for a caravan which is the occupier's main or only home.
Shop	means any shop, store, stall or other place (including a vehicle or the consumer's home) at which goods, services, accommodation or facilities are offered to consumers.
Trader	means anyone (retailers, manufacturers, agents, service providers and others) who is acting in the course of a business.

Part 1: Price comparisons

1.1 Price comparisons generally

1.1.1 Always make the meaning of price indications clear. Do not leave consumers to guess whether or not a price comparison is being made. If no price comparison is intended, do not use words or phrases which, in their normal, everyday use and in the context in which they are used, are likely to give your customers the impression that a price comparison is being made.

1.1.2 Price comparisons should always state the higher price as well as the price you intend to charge for the product (goods, services, accommodation or facilities). Do not make statements like 'sale price £5' or 'reduced to £39' without quoting the higher price to which they refer.

1.1.3 It should be clear what sort of price the higher price is. For example, comparisons with something described by words like 'regular price', 'usual price' or 'normal price' should say whose regular, usual or normal price it is (eg 'our normal price'). Descriptions like 'reduced from' and crossed out higher prices should be used only if they refer to your own previous price. Words should not be used in price indications other than with their normal everyday meanings.

1.1.4 Do not use initials or abbreviations to describe the higher price in a comparison, except for the initials 'RRP' to describe a recommended retail price or the abbreviation 'man rec price' to describe a manufacturer's recommended price (see paragraph 1.6.2 below).

1.1.5 Follow the part of the code (sections 1.2 to 1.6 as appropriate) which applies to the type of comparison you intend to make.

1.2 Comparisons with the trader's own previous price

General

1.2.1 In any comparison between your present selling price and another price at which you have in the past offered the product, you should state the previous price as well as the new lower price.

1.2.2 In any comparison with your own previous price:

(a) the previous price should be the last price at which the product was available to consumers in the previous 6 months;

(b) the product should have been available to consumers at that price for at least 28 consecutive days in the previous 6 months; and

(c) the previous price should have applied (as above) for that period at the same shop where the reduced price is now being offered.

The 28 days at (b) above may include bank holidays Sundays or other days of religious observance when the shop was closed; and up to 4 days when, for reasons beyond your control, the product was not available for supply. The product must not have been offered at a different price between that 28-day period and the day when the reduced price is first offered.

1.2.3 If the previous price in a comparison does not meet one or more of the conditions set out in paragraph 1.2.2 above:

(i) the comparison should be fair and meaningful; and

(ii) give a clear and positive explanation of the period for which and the circumstances in which that higher price applied.

For example 'these goods were on sale here at the higher price from 1 February to 26 February' or 'these goods were on sale at the higher price in 10 of our 95 stores only'. Display the explanation clearly, and as prominently as the price indication. You should not use general disclaimers saying for example that the higher prices used in comparisons have not necessarily applied for 28 consecutive days.

Food, drink and perishable goods

1.2.4 For any food and drink, you need not give a positive explanation if the previous price in a comparison has not applied for 28 consecutive days, provided it was the last price at which the goods were on sale in the previous 6 months and applied in the same shop where the reduced price is now being offered. This also applies to non-food perishables, if they have a shelf-life of less than six weeks.

Catalogue and mail order traders

1.2.5 Where products are sold only through a catalogue, advertisement or leaflet, any comparison with a previous price should be with the price in your own last catalogue, advertisement or leaflet. If you sell the same products both in shops and through catalogues etc, the previous price should be the last price at which you offered the product. You should also follow the guidance in paragraphs 1.2.2 (a) and (b). If your price comparison does not meet these conditions, you should follow the guidance in paragraph 1.2.3.

Making a series of reductions

1.2.6 If you advertise a price reduction and then want to reduce the price further during the same sale or special offer period, the intervening price (or prices) need not have applied for 28 days. In these circumstances unless you use a positive explanation (paragraph 1.2.3):

> the highest price in the series must have applied for 28 consecutive days in the last 6 months at the same shop: and

> you must show the highest price, the intervening price(s) and the current selling price (eg £~~40~~, £~~20~~, £~~10~~, £5').

1.3 Introductory offers, after-sale or after-promotion prices

Introductory Offers

1.3.1 Do not call a promotion an introductory offer unless you intend to continue to offer the product for sale after the offer period is over and to do so at a higher price.

1.3.2 Do not allow an offer to run on so long that it becomes misleading to describe it as an introductory or other special offer. What is a reasonable period will depend on the circumstances (but, depending on the shelf-life of the product, it is likely to be a matter of weeks, not months). An offer is unlikely to be misleading if you state the date the offer will end and keep to it. If you then extend the offer period, make it clear that you have done so.

Quoting a future price

1.3.3 If you indicate an after-sale or after-promotion price, do so only if you are certain that, subject only to circumstances beyond your control, you will continue to offer identical products at that price for at least 28 days in the 3 months after the end of the offer period or after the offer stocks run out.

1.3.4 If you decide to quote a future price, write what you mean in full. Do not use initials to describe it (eg 'ASP', 'APP'). The description should be clearly and prominently displayed, with the price indication.

1.4 Comparisons with prices related to different circumstances

1.4.1 This section covers comparisons with prices:

(a) for different quantities (eg '15p each, 4 for 50p');

(b) for goods in a different condition (eg 'seconds £20, when perfect £30');

(c) for a different availability (eg 'price £50, price when ordered specially £60');

(d) for goods in a totally different state (eg 'price in kit form £50, price ready-assembled £70'); or

(e) for special groups of people (eg 'senior citizens' price £2.50, others £5').

General

1.4.2 Do not make such comparisons unless the product is available in the different quantity, conditions etc at the price you quote. Make clear to consumers the different circumstances which apply and show them prominently with the price indication. Do not use initials (eg 'RAP' for 'ready-assembled price') to describe the different circumstances, but write what you mean in full.

'When perfect' comparisons

1.4.3 If you do not have the perfect goods on sale in the same shop:

(a) follow section 1.2 if the 'when perfect' price is your own previous price for the goods;

(b) follow section 1.5 if the 'when perfect' price is another trader's price; or

(c) follow section 1.6 if the 'when perfect' price is one recommended by the manufacturer or supplier.

Goods in a different state

1.4.4 Only make comparisons with goods in a totally different state if:

(a) a reasonable proportion (say a third (by quantity)) of your stock of those goods is readily available for sale to consumers in that different state (for example, ready assembled) at the quoted price and from the shop where the price comparison is made; *or*

(b) another trader is offering those goods in that state at the quoted price and you follow section 1.5 below.

Prices for special groups of people

1.4.5 If you want to compare different prices which you charge to different groups of people (eg one price for existing customers and another for new customers, or one price for people who are members of a named organisation (other than the trader) and another for those who are not), do not use words like 'our normal' or 'our regular' to describe the higher price, unless it applies to at least half your customers.

1.5 Comparisons with another trader's prices

1.5.1 Only compare your prices with another trader's price if :

(a) you know that his price which you quote is accurate and up-to-date;

(b) you give the name of the other trader clearly and prominently, with the price comparison;

(c) you identify the shop where the other trader's price applies, if that other trader is a retailer; and

(d) the other trader's price which you quote applies to the same products – or to substantially similar products and you state any differences clearly.

1.5.2 Do not make statements like 'if you can buy this product elsewhere for less, we will refund the difference' about your 'own brand' products which other traders do not stock, unless your offer will also apply to other traders' equivalent goods. If there are any conditions attached to the offer (eg it only applies to goods on sale in the same town) you should show them clearly and prominently, with the statement.

1.6 Comparisons with 'Recommended Retail Price' or similar

General

1.6.1 This section covers comparisons with recommended retail prices, manufacturers' recommended prices, suggested retail prices, suppliers' suggested retail prices and similar descriptions. It also covers prices given to co-operative and voluntary group organisations by their wholesalers or headquarters organisations.

1.6.2 Do not use initials or abbreviations to describe the higher price in a comparison *unless*:

(a) you use the initials 'RRP' to describe a recommended retail price; or

(b) you use the abbreviation 'man rec price' to describe a manufacturer's recommended price.

Write all other descriptions out in full and show them clearly and prominently with the price indication.

1.6.3 Do not use a recommended price in a comparison unless:

(a) it has been recommended to you by the manufacturer or supplier as a price at which the product might be sold to consumers;

(b) you deal with that manufacturer or supplier on normal commercial terms. (This will generally be the case for members of cooperative or voluntary group organisations in relation to their wholesalers or headquarters organisations); and

(c) the price is not significantly higher than prices at which the product is generally sold at the time you first make that comparison.

1.7 Pre-printed prices

1.7.1 Make sure you pass on to consumers any reduction stated on the manufacturer's packaging (eg 'flash packs' such as '10p off RRP').

1.7.2 You are making a price comparison if goods have a clearly visible price already printed on the packaging which is higher than the price you will charge for them. Such pre-printed prices are, in effect, recommended prices (except for retailers' own label goods) and you should follow paragraphs 1.6.1 to 1.6.4. You need not state that the price is a recommended price.

1.8 References to value or worth

1.8.1 Do not compare your prices with an amount described only as 'worth' or 'value'.

1.8.2 Do not present general advertising slogans which refer to 'value' or 'worth' in a way which is likely to be seen by consumers as a price comparison.

1.9 Sales or special events

1.9.1 If you have bought in items specially for a sale, and you make this clear, you should not quote a higher price when indicating that they are special purchases. Otherwise, your price indications for individual items in the sale which are reduced should comply with section 1.1 of the Code and whichever of sections 1.2 to 1.6 applies to the type of comparison you are making.

1.9.2 If you just have a general notice saying, for example, that all products are at 'half marked price', the marked price on the individual items should be your own previous price and you should follow section 1.2 of the Code.

182 Appendix 2

1.9.3 Do not use general notices saying, eg 'up to 50% off' unless the maximum reduction quoted applies to at least 10% (by quantity) of the range of products on offer.

1.10 Free offers

1.10.1 Make clear to consumers, at the time of the offer for sale, exactly what they will have to buy to get the 'free offer'.

1.10.2 If you give any indication of the monetary value of the 'free offer', and that sum is not your own present price for the product, follow whichever of sections 1.2 to 1.6 covers the type of price it is.

1.10.3 If there are any conditions attached to the 'free offer', give at least the main points of those conditions with the price indication and make clear to consumers where, before they are committed to buy, they can get full details of the conditions.

1.10.4 Do not claim that an offer is free if:

(a) you have imposed additional charges that you would not normally make;

(b) you have inflated the price of any product the consumer must buy or the incidental charges (for example, postage) the consumer must pay to get the 'free offer'; or

(c) you will reduce the price to consumers who do not take it up.

Part 2: Actual price to consumer

2.1 Indicating two different prices

2.1.1 The Consumer Protection Act makes it an offence to indicate a price for goods or services which is lower than the one that actually applies, for example, showing one price in an advertisement, window display, shelf marking or on the item itself, and then charging a higher price at the point of sale or checkout.

2.2 Incomplete information and non-optional extras

2.2.1 Make clear in your price indications the full price consumers will have to pay for the product. Some examples of how to do so in particular circumstances are set out below.

Limited availability of product

2.2.2 Where the price you are quoting for products only applies to a limited number of, say, orders, sizes or colours, you should make this clear in your price indication (eg 'available in other colours or sizes at additional cost').

Prices relating to differing forms of products

2.2.3 If the price you are quoting for particular products does not apply to the products in the form they are displayed or advertised, say so clearly in your price indication. For example, advertisements for self-assembly furniture and the like should make it clear that the price refers to a kit of parts.

Postage, packing and delivery charges

2.2.4 If you sell by mail order, make clear any additional charges for postage, packing or delivery on the order form or similar document, so that consumers are fully aware of them before being committed to buying. Where you cannot determine these charges in advance, show clearly on the order form how they will be calculated (eg 'Post Office rates apply'), or the place in the catalogue etc where the information is given.

2.2.5 If you sell goods from a shop and offer a delivery service for certain items, make it clear whether there are any separate delivery charges (eg for delivery outside a particular area) and what those charges are, before the consumer is committed to buying.

Value Added Tax

(i) Price indications to consumers

2.2.6 All price indications you give to private consumers, by whatever means, should include VAT.

(ii) Price indications to business customers

2.2.7 Prices may be indicated exclusive of VAT in shops where or advertisements from which most of your business is with business customers. If you also carry out business with private consumers at those shops or from those advertisements you should make clear that the prices exclude VAT and:

(i) display VAT-inclusive prices with equal prominence, or

(ii) display prominent statements that on top of the quoted price customers will also have to pay VAT at 15% (or the current rate).

(iii) Professional fees

2.2.8 Where you indicate a price (including estimates) for a professional fee, make clear what it covers. The price should generally include VAT. In cases where the fee is based on an as-yet-unknown sum of money (for example, the sale price of a house), either:

(i) quote a fee which includes VAT; or

(ii) make it clear that in additon to your fee the consumer would have to pay VAT at the current rate (eg 'fee of 1½% of purchase price, plus VAT at 15%).

Make sure that whichever method you choose is used for both estimates and final bills.

(iv) Building work

2.2.9 In estimates for building work, either include VAT in the price indication or indicate with equal prominence the amount or rate of VAT payable in addition to your basic figure. If you give a separate amount for VAT, make it clear that if any provisional sums in estimates vary then the amount of VAT payable would also vary.

Service, cover and minimum charges in hotels, restaurants and similar establishments

2.2.10 If your customers in hotels, restaurants or similar places must pay a non-optional extra charge, eg a 'service':

(i) incorporate the charge within fully inclusive prices wherever practicable; and

(ii) display the fact clearly on any price list or priced menu, whether displayed inside or outside (eg by using statements like 'all prices include service').

Do not include suggested optional sums, whether for service or any other item, in the bill presented to the customer.

2.2.11 It will not be practical to include some non-optional extra charges in a quoted price; for instance, if you make a flat charge per person or per table in a restaurant (often referred to as a 'cover charge') or a minimum charge. In such cases the charge should be shown as prominently as other prices on any list or menu, whether displayed inside or outside.

Holiday and travel prices

2.2.12 If you offer a variety of prices to give consumers a choice, (for example, paying more or less for a holiday depending on the time of year or the standard of accommodation), make clear in your brochure – or any other price indication – what the basic price is and what it covers. Give details of any optional additional charges and what those charges cover, or of the place where this information can be found, clearly and close to the basic price.

2.2.13 Any non-optional extra charges which are for fixed amounts should be included in the basic price and not shown as additions, unless they are only payable by some consumers. In that case you should specify, near to the details of the basic price, either what the amounts are and the circumstances in which they are payable, or where in the brochure etc the information is given.

2.2.14 Details of non-optional extra charges which may vary, (such as holiday insurance) or of where in the brochure etc the information is given should be made clear to consumers near to the basic price.

2.2.15 If you reserve the right to increase prices after consumers have made their booking, state this clearly with all indications of prices, and include prominently in your brochure full information on the circumstances in which a surcharge is payable.

Ticket prices

2.2.16 If you sell tickets, whether for sporting events, cinema, theatre etc and your prices are higher than the regular price that would be charged to the public at the box office, ie higher than the 'face value', you should make clear in any price indication what the 'face value' of the ticket is.

Call-out charges

2.2.17 If you make a minimum call-out charge or other flat-rate charge (for example, for plumbing, gas or electrical appliance repairs etc carried out in consumers' homes) ensure that the consumer is made aware of the charge and whether the actual price may be higher (eg if work takes longer than a specific time) before being committed to using your services.

Credit facilities

2.2.18 Price indications about consumer credit should comply with the relevant requirements of regulations under the Consumer Credit Act 1974 governing the form and content of advertisements.

Insurance

2.2.19 Where actual premium rates for a particular consumer or the availability of insurance cover depend on an individual assessment, this should be made clear when any indication of the premium or the method of determining it is given to consumers.

Part 3: Price indications which become misleading after they have been given

3.1 General

3.1.1 The Consumer Protection Act makes it an offence to give a price indication which, although correct at the time, becomes misleading after you have given it, if:

(i) consumers could reasonably be expected still to be relying on it; and

(ii) you do not take reasonable steps to prevent them doing so.

Clearly it will not be necessary or even possible in many instances to inform all those who may have been given the misleading price indication. However, you should always make sure consumers are given the correct information before they are committed to buying a product and be prepared to cancel any transaction which a consumer has entered into on the basis of a price indication which has become misleading.

3.1.2 Do not give price indications which you know or intend will only apply for a limited period, without making this fact clear in the advertisement or price indication.

3.1.3 The following paragraphs set out what you should do in some particular circumstances.

3.2 Newspaper and magazine advertisements

3.2.1 If the advertisement does not say otherwise, the price indication should apply for a reasonable period (as a general guide, at least 7 days or until the next issue of the newspaper or magazine in which the advertisement was published, whichever is longer). If the price indication becomes misleading within this period make sure consumers are given the correct information before they are committed to buying the product.

3.3 Mail order advertisements, catalogues and leaflets

3.3.1 Paragraph 3.2.1 above also applies to the time for which price indications in mail order advertisements and in regularly published catalogues or brochures should apply. If a price indication becomes misleading within this period, make the correct price indication clear to anyone who orders the product to which it relates. Do so before the consumer is committed to buying the product and, wherever practicable, before the goods are sent to the consumer.

3.4 Selling through agents

Holiday brochures and travel agents

3.4.1 Surcharges are covered in paragraph 2.2.15 above. If a price indication becomes misleading for any other reason, tour operators who sell direct to consumers should follow paragraph 3.3.1 above; and tour operators who sell through travel agents should follow paragraphs 3.4.2 and 3.4.3 below.

3.4.2 If a price indication becomes misleading while your brochure is still current, make this clear to the travel agents to whom you distributed the brochure. Be prepared to cancel any holiday bookings consumers have made on the basis of a misleading price indication.

3.4.3 In the circumstances set out in paragraph 3.4.2, travel agents should ensure that the correct price indication is made clear to consumers before they make a booking.

Insurance and independent intermediaries

3.4.4 Insurers who sell their products through agents or independent intermediaries should take all reasonable steps to ensure that all such agents who are known to hold information on the insurer's premium rates and terms of the cover provided are told clearly of any changes in those rates or terms.

3.4.5 Agents, independent intermediaries and providers of quotation systems should ensure that they act on changes notified to them by an insurer.

3.5 Changes in the rate of value added tax

3.5.1 If your price indications become misleadmg because of a change in the general rate of VAT, or other taxes paid at point of sale, make the correct price indication clear to any consumers who order products. Do so before the consumer is committed to buying the product and, wherever practicable, before the goods are sent to the consumer.

Part 4: Sale of new homes

4.1 A 'new home' is any building, or part of a building to be used only as a private dwelling which is either:

(i) a newly-built house or flat; or

(ii) a newly-converted existing building which has not previously been used in that form as a private home.

4.2 The Consumer Protection Act and this Code apply to new homes which are either for sale freehold or covered by a long lease, ie with more than 21 years to run. In this context the term 'trader' covers not only a business vendor, such as a developer, but also an estate agent acting on behalf of such a vendor.

4.3 You should follow the relevant provision of Part 1 of the Code if:

(i) you want to make a comparison between the price at which you offer new homes for sale and any other price;

(ii) you offer an inclusive price for new homes which also covers such items as furnishings, domestic appliances and insurance and you compare their value with, for example, High Street prices for similar items.

4.4 Part 2 of the Code gives details of the provisions you should follow if:

(i) the new houses you are selling, or any goods or services which apply to them, are only available in limited numbers or range;

(ii) the sale price you give does not apply to the houses as displayed; or

(iii) there are additional non-optional charges payable.

APPENDIX 3

NOTES FOR GUIDANCE ON COUPONS – RECOMMENDED BEST PRACTICE

Published by, and reproduced here with the permission of, the Institute of Sales Promotion, Arena House, 66–68 Pentonville Road, Islington, London N1 9HS. Tel: 0171–837 5340; Fax: 0171–837 5326.

Jointly produced and endorsed by The Article Number Association; The British Retail Consortium; The Federation of Wholesale Distributors; The Food and Drink Federation; The Institute of Sales Promotion.

First published January 1994.

192   Appendix 3

When a coupon is issued it is handled by distribution media, the public, retailers and clearing houses. Accordingly, consumers must be clear that they are being offered an opportunity to save money on a product; retailers are relied upon to accept coupons and give consumers the correct saving and it is in the interest of all promoters to ensure that their coupons can be processed quickly and efficiently by both retailers and clearing houses.

Anyone responsible for the design and/or issue of a coupon that is intended to be redeemed through the retail or wholesale trade should refer to these Notes for Guidance to ensure that all coupons adhere to the basic requirements of good coupon design.

Closing dates

Value

Size and shape

Instructions

Bar code

Product details

- Where coupons are only redeemable at specified outlets, the store name should be clearly stated.
- Manufacturer or handling house code (if required).

a) These Notes for Guidance cover the accepted basic requirements for a coupon which gives 'money-off' a nominated product and which is designed to be redeemed through the retailer or wholesale trade. They outline its design, size, redemption and handling requirements.

b) They have been prepared jointly by the Article Number Association, the British Retail Consortium, the Food and Drink Federation, the Institute of Sales Promotion and have been endorsed by the Federation of Wholesale Distribution and are accepted by these bodies as standard practice.

c) Special uses of coupons, such as alternative value coupons and those requiring 'proof of purchase' to be attached, are more difficult to handle, therefore, special conditions are likely to apply in relation to handling costs, to be negotiated on an individual company basis at the time of the promotion. These types of coupon are, however, still subject to these Notes for Guidance.

Closing dates

- Where an offer closing date is applied, this should be clearly and prominently marked using the words 'Valid until . . .'

- Promoters should redeem coupons from retailers up to *at least six months* beyond any stated consumer closing date, but a retailer closing date should *not* appear on the coupon.

- See also section concerning on-pack coupons.

Value

- The sterling value should appear once as a bold figure on the front face.

- For a double sided coupon, the value should only appear once on each face and in such a manner that the coupon could not be divided or tendered in two pieces.

- The word 'COUPON' or 'VOUCHER' should appear next to or near the stated value.

- The words 'OFF NEXT PURCHASE' should appear in one bold typeface.

Size and shape

- Rectangular
- Minimum size: 4cm x 8cm
- Maximum size: 7cm x 13cm

Coupons incorporated in printed matter

- Where coupons are incorporated in other print matter (eg magazines/leaflets), the coupon must be easy to detach.

- A clear indication around the border of the coupon itself should appear as dotted or 'cut' lines.

- Check that the coupon is not printed on the reverse of another coupon, or on the reverse of any other bar code.

- Care should be taken to ensure that any copy in printed matter that refers to the coupon cannot be construed as being an additional coupon.

Bar code

- All coupons that are intended for general redemption should carry a bar code.

- Each different coupon promotion requires a different bar code symbol to encode its reference number and value; each different offer closing date must have a different bar code.

- The bar code should be printed wherever possible on white, and depending on the print process, at a size of at least 100% (26.26mm x 37.29mm). This includes the light margins which surround the bar code, and are safeguarded by the leading digit 9 on the left hand side and the light margin chevron on the right hand side. Key lines should not be printed near the bar code, as this may cause difficulties when the bar code is scanned.

- The value encoded in the bar code should be the same as the face value of the coupon.

- The bar code, including its surrounding light margins, should be located at least 10mm from the base and right hand edge of the coupon.

- Coupon issuer numbers, which are not the same as company prefix numbers, are supplied by the Article Number Association, 11 Kingsway, London, WC2B 6AR, tel 0171–836 3398. Numbers are only issued to ANA member companies and a charge for issue is made.

Instructions

- Coupons should carry clear instructions to both consumer and trade on usage and redemption. Consumer instructions should be worded along the following lines: 'This coupon can only be used as part payment for (Brand/Product). Only one coupon can be used against each item purchased. Please do not attempt to redeem this coupon against any other product as refusal to accept may cause embarrassment and delay at the checkout.'

- The promoter's name and the redemption address should be clearly stated.

Product details

- The product(s) and if applicable, size(s) should be stated clearly and conspicuously.

Additional considerations for on-pack coupons

- Care should be taken to ensure that the coupon bar code is not visible at the time of product purchase. This is to avoid potential confusion at the checkout.

- Promoters should ensure that coupons which are attached to labels or direct to packages are properly secured to prevent loss, yet remain detachable.

- Coupons should be situated so as not to become soiled or stained by either direct contact with, or use of, the product.

- Where coupons are embodied as part of a special pack and are to be redeemed against the next purchase, the words 'off next purchase' should appear in one bold typeface, size and colour.

- Careful consideration should be given as to the desirability of a closing date, especially where the product carries an extended 'minimum durability' date.

- When on-pack coupons coincide with any other kind of special on-pack price or money-off marking applied by the promoter, then one should be clearly differentiated from the other.

Free product coupons

- Where there is an intention to provide consumers with a coupon for the entire purchase price of a product, special care is needed. Promoters wishing to issue free product coupons are advised to consult their retail customers before issue.

Trade notification

- Promoters should notify their trade customers in advance of their intention to issue on-pack coupons. It is also advisable to notify the trade in advance of major off-pack coupon campaigns.

- Outer cases containing coupon packs should be readily identfied as such.

- During a 'cross-couponing' or 'off next purchase' campaign, particularly if the coupon is against another brand, promoters should, wherever possible, make the brand available in regular packs to their trade customers and inform them that these packs are available.

Handling allowances

- Where promotional schemes take the form of coupons redeemable through the trade, an agreed allowance should be given to cover sorting, counting and collections etc. An annual benchmark figure is agreed between the Food and Drink Federation and the British Retail Consortium.

Materials

- Coupons should be printed on durable material of a weight and texture which is easy to handle without coupons sticking together or ripping. Materials such as polythene or cellophane are feasible although special care will be needed to ensure that the bar code will scan. The use of unusual materials for coupons should be discussed with both trade customers and the clearing house prior to production.

Appendix 4

THE INSTITUTE OF SALES PROMOTION: PROMOTIONAL HANDLING CODE OF PRACTICE

First edition November 1988; this edition 1994

Published by, and reproduced here with permission of, the Institute of Sales Promotion, 66-68 Pentonville Road, Islington, London N1 9HS. Tel: 0171–837 5340

Preface

Sales promotions is, of course, a well-developed tool of marketing, and continues to develop and grow in significance.

In this context it is vitally necessary that sales promotion gives a fair deal to consumers and is seen to give a fair deal. This principle must exist all the way through the sales promotion process, involving the idea, the graphics, the copy, the communication, and, of course, the fulfilment and handling aspect.

This Code of Practice, therefore, represents a commitment by the Promotional Handling Association, to play its part in the achievement of an overall fair deal in sales promotion terms. Not only is this important in the specific sense, but adherence by all parties to the code is important in demonstrating that self-regulation can, and does, work and is highly preferable to cumbersome legislation.

This Code features strongly the need for a high level of co-operation with and from, our clients and calls for a high degree of consultation in the planning stages, culminating in a specific and detailed brief.

We feel that it is important that the code should be applied, not only to the letter, but also in the spirit in which it is intended.

Richard Lewis

Chairman of the Promotional Handling Association

January 1994

Contents

1	Introduction	209
2	The Promotional Handling Code	211
3	General Recommendations	213
4	Appendix A: Briefing Prompt List	215

1 Introduction

1.1 Objectives of the Code

This Code seeks to protect the interests of consumers, ISP members and others who use the services of handling fulfilment houses.

1.2 Administration and relationship of the Code

1.2.1 This Code is administered by the Institute of Sales Promotion (referred to hereafter as the ISP) and endorses without exception the Advertising Standards Authority and the British Code of Sales Promotion Practice, in conjunction with which it should be read. Both Codes are supported and upheld by all handling houses jointly in membership of the ISP and The Promotional Handling Association (PHA hereafter). The membership of the PHA will elect bi-annually a representative to a permanent place on the services sub-committee of the ISP.

1.2.2 The ISP in conjunction with the PHA will maintain a directory of handling houses that are members of both bodies. The day-to-day administration of the directory will be the responsibility of the ISP services sub-committee and the PHA, who will jointly ensure that good order and housekeeping are maintained.

1.3 Commitment to The Promotional Handling Code

Adoption of the Code by a handling house represents a commitment to respect and uphold the confidence placed in the handling house by those who contract services to it.

1.4 Definitions

1.4.1 In the context of this Code, '*handling houses*' is defined as an ISP/PHA member whose business is to receive or despatch on behalf of its clients to or from consumer or trade applicants redemptions for promotions, competitions, mailings, money-off coupons, or other types of fulfilment.

1.4.2 Similarly, the term 'client' is deemed to mean promoter, consultant, advertising agency or any other party acting as the principal in placing promotional handling business with the handling house.

1.4.3 The terms 'promoter', 'consumer' and 'product/s' used in this Code are as specified in section 3 of The British Code of Sales Promotion Practice.

1.5 Consumer interest

The Code recognises that all sales promotion should deal fairly and honourably with consumers and should be seen to do so. No handling house engaged in the conduct of a promotion should for its part abuse the trust of consumers or exploit their lack of experience or knowledge to their detriment.

1.6 Spirit of the Code

This Code is lo be applied in spirit as well as in the letter with the aim of precluding practices which might lead sales promotion into disrepute.

1.7 Briefing

This Code acknowledges that an accurate and detailed initial brief is fundamental to the efficient handling of any promotion and is the responsibility of the client in conjunction with the best endeavours of the handling house. As a guideline, a briefing prompt list is attached as Appendix A to this Code.

2 The Promotional Handling Code of Practice

2.1 Conduct

The handling house will conduct its business affairs in an ethical and professional manner with the intention to give satisfaction to its clients and to consumers.

2.2 Briefing, Quotation and Sub-contracting

2.2.1 The handling house must use its best endeavours to obtain a complete service specification (see Appendix A of this Code) from the client against which a firm written quotation inclusive of all foreseeable costs will be supplied, together with any identifiable cost exclusions.

2.2.2 The quotation will specify any supplier costs (ie packing materials, envelopes, etc) which are subject to price variation within the duration of the promotion.

2.2.3 The quotation will also state the period for which the price/s hold good and will declare any significant elements of the promotion the handling house intends to sub-contract.

2.2.4 Requests for a quotation from a prospective client will be dealt with promptly and efficiently. The handling house will not issue a quotation for work it cannot competently handle considering its workload and operational limitations. If it cannot, or has no wish to undertake the fulfilment of the promotion, the prospective client will be promptly so informed.

2.3 Consumer satisfaction and protection

2.3.1 The handling house undertakes to notify the client of all relevant consumer correspondence relating to the promotion and to deal with this promptly and efficiently at the client's cost if so required by the client. Alternatively, the handling house must forward without delay the correspondence to the client for action.

2.3.2 Sales promotions should be fulfilled by the handling house so as not to cause avoidable disappointment or dissatisfaction to the consumer. If the terms of the offer cannot be honoured, particularly if fulfilment is delayed through lack of stock of the offered items, the handling house must strongly recommend the client to authorise the prompt mailing of delay notifications to all consumers whose requests cannot be fulfilled within the promised period, such delay mailings to be at client's cost.

2.3.3 In the interests of consumers the handling house will not bank consumers' cheques or postal orders if sufficient stock of the offered item/s is not immediately available to fulfil requests. Such cheques and postal orders will be held in suspense under appropriate security conditions pending the arrival of stock in sufficient quantity at the handling house.

2.3.4 The handling house should agree in writing with the client on the stock-handling levels appropriate to the actual or expected response to the promotion and carefully monitor and report stock issues on an ongoing basis to ensure that the client is aware of the available stock level at all times and of the need to replenish where appropriate.

2.4 Representation of services

The handling house will not advertise, publicise or present its services in a misleading or deceptive manner.

2.5 Ownership of data

The handling house accepts that all names and addresses and other personal data accruing from a promotion are the sole property of the promoter and undertakes that they will not be used by the handling house or released to a third party for any purpose whatsoever other than the proper fulfilment of the promotion in accordance with the agreed brief or as otherwise directed in writing by the promoter or his authorised agent.

2.6 Confidentiality

The handling house and its staff will take the measures necessary to maintain absolute confidentiality at all times and will not reveal to a third party any details of the performance of any promotion or task without the written permission of the client.

2.7 Illegal or unacceptable promotions

The handling house may refuse involvement in, or withdraw immediately from, any promotion that it knows to be deceptive, illegal or contrary to The British Code of Sales Promotion Practice. The contract for any such promotion will be deemed null and void and any outstanding charges invoiced in full.

2.8 Accuracy of information

The handling house warrants that the information and reports it supplies to the client will be accurate and up to date to the best of its ability and belief.

2.9 Audit

2.9.1 Where a handling house is required to open a special bank account on behalf of a client, the handling house shall accept full responsibility for the proper conduct of the account and the accurate reconciliation of all monies credited or debited to it.

2.9.2 The handling house accepts full accountability for any postal or other cash floats held on behalf of a client and undertakes to notify the client immediately these fall below a previously agreed level; the handling house also warrants that it will reconcile and refund any surplus monies to the client promptly at the end of the promotion.

2.9.3 The handling house will maintain a full audit trail of all transactions in accordance with the agreed brief. By prior arrangement, the client or his representative may during normal working hours have access to the premises and records of the handling house to such extent as may be necessary to inspect stocks and validate the records relating to the client's promotion.

2.10 Notification of problems

2.10.1 The handling house will immediately and openly notify the client of any operational problem likely to affect the smooth running of the promotion in conformity with the agreed brief.

2.10.2 The cost of consumer correspondence arising from such a problem shall be borne by the handling house if the clear cause of the problem is the error or negligence of the handling house.

2.11 Destruction of client goods or materials

2.11.1 Except as provided for below, the handling house will not destroy or dispose of any goods or materials relating to a promotion without the prior written authority of the client.

2.11.2 The handling house reserves the right to destroy or otherwise dispose of any goods or materials which it deems to be hazardous or noxious.

2.11.3 A formal procedure should be agreed between handling house and client to cover the destruction or return to client of goods and materials following the closing date of a promotion. The procedure should cover destruction, return to client or arranged storage at a fee to be agreed.

2.12 Handling of competing products and services

Excepting for the redemption of money-off coupons submitted by the retail and wholesale trades, the handling house will not knowingly accept promotions or other tasks for competitive products or services without the prior knowledge and agreement of the clients concerned.

2.13 Relationship with client

The handling house will strive for a close working relationship with the client before, during and after the promotion. This should include the offer of assistance in planning, guidance on the application format and help with final evaluation/analysis.

3 General recommendations

3.1 Application forms

3.1.1 The design and legibility of the application form/coupon received by the handling house is a critical factor in the efficient handling of the promotion. Consumers must be able to complete the application in an easy and efficient manner ensuring that all relevant information is clearly stated. In certain cases practical considerations (ie pack size or materials) limit the specification outlined below. However, the handling house should urge its clients in their mutual interest to adhere to the following specification as closely as possible:

PLEASE PRINT IN CAPITAL LETTERS

1 Title (Mr/Mrs/Miss/Ms). . . .

2 Initials. . . .

3 Surname. . . .

4 Address line 1. . . .

5 Address line 2. . . .

6 Town. . . .

7 County. . . .

8 Postcode. . . .

9 Date. . . .

10 Telephone number. . . .

11 Payment type (cheque/postal order/cash/credit card). . . .

12 Payment value £. . . .

13 Credit card no, signature and card expiry date. . . .

14 No of POPs submitted. . . .

15 Variable order details (ie quantity/size/colour). . . .

16 Pre-printed media source code. . . .

17 Geographic limitations, if any (ie; offers restricted to England & Wales). . . .

Items 1–9 are essential information, as is the request to print in capitals

Items 10–16 only if appropriate to the promotion.

3.1.2 The handling house recognises the importance of postcode usage by consumers and will promote to its clients the benefits of encouraging applicants to quote their postcodes.

3.2 Systems and procedures

These constitute an inherent part of the handling and fulfilment operation. Considerable variation exists between each handling house and, therefore, strict guidelines are impossible to lay down. However, the handling house must ensure that all applications are processed in the most efficient manner to meet each clients' brief and within the period specified in the offer. The systems and procedures used for a specific client shall be available for inspection by that client by prior arrangement provided this does not contravene the Code, The British Code of Sales Promotion Practice, or the confidentiality of information belonging to any other client.

3.3 Briefing procedure

It is imperative that the client supplies all details relevant to a promotion *at least four weeks* before start date. The handling house and client should use a briefing form or check list (see guidelines, Appendix A) to ensure that every aspect of the fulfilment requirement is understood and priced. It is in the mutual interest of both parties that this is subsequently confirmed by way of written quotation or contract, whichever is appropriate.

3.4 Data protection

3.4.1 If a client uses the handling house's computer facilities for the capture and storage of names and addresses or other personal information, the handling house (in its capacity as a bureau) and the client (and ultimate list owner if not the client) are required to conform to the provisions of the Data Protection Act and must register as appropriate with the Registrar.

3.4.2 To reiterate paragraph 2.6 of this Code: such information is the sole property of the promoter (or ultimate list owner). It is the responsibility of the handling house to implement procedures by which masterfile information, either held on-line within the handling house's computer system or archived to magnetic or other media, is kept under secure conditions and in a manner to facilitate retrieval within forty days when required by the client or a consumer as provided for by the Data Protection Act. The handling house will observe the data security and back-up procedures as laid down by the National Computing Centre.

3.4.3 Aggregated information relating to response rates, type of promotion and seasonal variations may be used by the handling house for its own internal purposes or for commercial purposes, provided always that such use conforms with the provisions of this Code and the Data Protection Act and does not identify individual consumers, the client or the product promoted or otherwise breach client confidentiality.

APPENDIX A: Briefing prompt list

1 DESCRIPTION OF PROMOTION: incentive offered/instructions to applicant/special instructions (ie one per household)

2 HANDLING REQUIREMENT: handling mechanic/turnround time

3 PROMOTION DURATION: start date/close date

4 RESPONSE FORECAST: anticipated volume/response pattern

5 PROMOTION MEDIA: on-pack/off the page/TV/direct mail etc

6 APPLICATION FORMAT: coupons / leaflet / plain paper / telephone

7 POP REQUIREMENT: number / type / tolerances / count procedures

8 PAYMENT REQUIREMENT: amount(s) / coins / cheques / postal orders / credit cards / charge cards / tolerances / await cheque clearance

9 BANK ACCOUNT: client's or handling house: if latter specify charges levied by bank for (a) paying-in and (b) clearance of cheques

10 POSTAGE & DESPATCH: 1st class mail / 2nd class / rebate / Trakback (recorded delivery) / registered mail / carrier / postage

float / direct charge to client's own postal account

11 PACKING MATERIALS: delivered pre-packed / envelope / padded bag / carton / other

12 STORAGE REQUIREMENT: quantities / period / security or general

13 INSURANCE OF GOODS: handling house or client

14 CAPTURE AND PRODUCTION OF APPLICATION DETAILS: manual or computer / fields required / duplication / selections / sortations

15 REPORTS AND ANALYSES: type/frequency/period covered

16 CONSUMER RELATIONS: procedures for incorrect applications/correspondence/complaints/returns/exchanges/refunds

17 AUDIT: POP & application retention/record despatch date

18 STOCK CONTROL: re-order levels/returns/final disposal

19 GOODS INWARD: delivery dates(s) / counting-in procedure / advice of receipts to client

20 SECURITY/CONFIDENTIALITY: special requirements

APPENDIX 5

INCORPORATED SOCIETY OF BRITISH ADVERTISERS: TRADE INCENTIVES – GOOD AND BAD PRACTICE

Published by, and reproduced here with the permission of, The Incorporated Society of British Advertisers Ltd, 44 Hertford Street, London W1Y 8AE. Tel: 0171–499 7502; Fax: 0171–629 5355.

Manufacturers in many industries use incentives – additional rewards in cash or kind on top of their normal trade margins – to persuade the trade, or sections of it, to give active support to their products (to stock, to display, to advertisers, to promote, to reduce price etc, supply between manufacturer and consumer to operate more efficiently. They are then a valuable marketing tool which can work in the economic interest of the consumer and such incentives represent unexceptionable trading practice.

However, some incentive techniques, when *not* properly directed and administered, can act to distort competition and, in the extreme case, can result in criminal acts. When cash or value items are concerned, trade incentives can also have important tax implications for the recipient. The purpose of this note is to draw attention to certain generally accepted principles of good practice to help ISBA members to ensure that they are understood at all levels in their management structure. It may also serve as a reminder of the dangers which board members run when salesmen's practices are not adequately controlled.

The difference between the admissible and the inadmissible has been the subject of much sophisticated argument (often exemplified by numbers of bottles of whisky!) Nonetheless, two simple guiding lights burn brightly.

Firstly, the limits of legally permissible action are prescribed by the Public Bodies Corrupt Practices Act 1889 and the Prevention of

Corruption Act 1906. In principle, no incentive may be offered to any public servant under any circumstances. Similarly, no gift or benefit of material value to the recipient may be offered to employees in the private sector – but, in this case, the consent of the employer would avoid the commission of a crime.

Secondly, guidance about the limits of ethical practice in offering incentives to other people's employees is given in the ICC Code of Sales Promotion Practice, Article 12, repeated in the British Code of Sales Promotion Practice, Clause 43.

These Codes recognise the danger that trade promotions may lead to a conflict of loyalty because there is a clearly recognisable danger when incentives are offered to the personal gain rather than on proper commercial criteria. They therefore require that the prior permission of the employer, or his responsible manager, be obtained before valuable incentives are offered to any employee.

The existence of voluntary constraints on bad practice are encouraging and helpful, but will not itself eliminate bad practice without commitment at board level. We believe that the attached summary covers the key points which directors of ISBA members' companies should observe.

INCENTIVES TO OTHER PEOPLE'S EMPLOYEES – PRINCIPLES OF GOOD PRACTICE

1 A policy defining the proper use and administration of trade incentives should be laid down by the board *in writing*. It should make it clear that improper payments will not be sanctioned, or condoned, in any circumstances.

2 This policy should be well-known both internally and externally.

Internally it should be recognised that management will never be criticised for loss of business arising from adherence to the policy. *Externally*, knowledge of this policy will often provide the best protection against pressures for additional trade benefits.

3. Trade practices vary greatly but the policy may need to consider action under the following headings:

Normal distributive channels: no incentive (other than items of negligible value) should be offered to the trade without prior permission in writing, from a main board member of the customer concerned.

Public sector: steps should be taken to ensure that incentives offered to the distributive trade are not inadvertently, and illegally, offered to the public sector, either directly or indirectly. (Particularly important in the case of industrial and non-distributive trades.)

Cash or vouchers: cash or vouchers for cash present particular difficulties. All credits should be made out in the name of the company concerned and be routed through the office nominated by the customer.

Receipts: all individual payments to customers (or to consumers as a result of trade activity) should be acknowledged by a signature from the recipient.

Objectives: good practice depends upon clear-cut, and actionable performance objectives. Payment should be withheld for non-performance.

Records: accurate records should be kept of all trade incentive payments and awards. A summary should be passed to the main board member of the customer who initially agreed the incentive programme.

Inland Revenue: incentive payments, (including items of value) may have important tax implications for the recipient. This may, in turn, affect the goodwill of the promoter unless steps are taken, through prior discussion with the Inland Revenue, to mitigate this effect. The Inland Revenue may demand to see the records mentioned in the foregoing section.

Public relations: recent events have shown that occasional lapses from the standards suggested above have turned this into a sensitive area. Members are advised to nominate channels for dealing with any enquiries from media on this subject.

Review: trading practices and competitive pressures never stand still. Members are advised to institute an annual review at board level of the effectiveness of this policy.

APPENDIX 6

THE CHARTERED INSTITUTE OF PURCHASING AND SUPPLY: ETHICAL CODE

Published by, and reproduced here with permission of, the Chartered Institute of Purchasing and Supply, Easton House, Easton on the Hill, Stamford, Lincolnshire PE9 3NZ. Tel: 01780 56777

Introduction

1 In applying to join the Institute, members undertake to abide by 'the Constitution, Memorandum and Articles of Association, Rules and By-Laws of the Institute'. The Code set out below was approved by the Institute's Council on 26 February, 1977 and is binding on members.

2 The cases of members reported to have breached the Code shall be investigated by a Disciplinary Committee appointed by the Council; where a case is proven, a member may, depending on the circumstances and the gravity of the charge, be admonished, reprimanded, suspended from membership or removed from the list of members. Details of cases in which members are found in breach of the Code will be notified in the publications of the Institute.

Precepts

3 Members shall never use their authority or office for personal gain and shall seek to uphold and enhance the standing of the purchasing and supply profession and the Institute by:

(a) maintaining an unimpeachable standard of integrity in all their business relationships both inside and outside the organisations in which they are employed;

(b) fostering the highest possible standards of professional competence amongst those for whom they are responsible;
(c) optimising the use of resources for which they are responsible to provide the maximum benefit to their employing organisation;
(d) complying both with the letter and the spirit of:
  (i) the law of the country in which they practise;
  (ii) such guidance on professional practice as may be issued by the Institute from time to time;
  (iii) contractual obligations;
(e) rejecting any business practice which might reasonably be deemed improper.

Guidance

4 In applying these precepts, members should follow the guidance set out below:

(a) *Declaration of interest* Any personal interest which may impinge or might reasonably be deemed by others to impinge on a member's impartiality in any matter relevant to his or her duties should be declared.
(b) *Confidentiality and accuracy of information* The confidentiality of information received in the course of duty should be respected and should never be used for personal gain; information given in the course of duty should be true and fair and never designed to mislead.
(c) *Competition* While bearing in mind the advantages to the member's employing organisation of maintaining a continuing relationship with a supplier, any arrangement which might, in the long term, prevent the effective operation of fair competition, should be avoided.
(d) *Business gifts* Business gifts other than items of very small intrinsic value such as business diaries or calendars should not be accepted.
(e) *Hospitality* Modest hospitality is an accepted courtesy of a business relationship. However, the recipient should not allow him or herself to reach a position whereby he or she might be or might be deemed by others to have been influenced in making a business decision as a consequence of accepting such hospitality; the frequency and scale of hospitality accepted

should not be significantly greater than the recipient's employer would be likely to provide in return.
(f) When it is not easy to decide between what is and is not acceptable in terms of gifts or hospitality, the offer should be declined or advice sought from the member's superior.

5 Advice on any aspect of the precepts and guidance set out above may be obtained on written request to the Institute.

Appendix 7

THE CHARTERED INSTITUTE OF PURCHASING AND SUPPLY: RULES FOR TRADE PROMOTIONS

Published by, and reproduced here with permission of, the Chartered Institute of Purchasing and Supply, Easton House, Easton on the Hill, Stamford, Lincolnshire PE9 3NZ. Tel: 01780 56777

Introduction

The CIPS Rules for Trade Promotions are designed to overcome the legal and ethical difficulties which arise when offers of personal incentives (vouchers, gifts, holidays, competition prizes etc) are used to promote the sale of goods or services.

Rules

1 It is illegal to offer personal material incentives to public employees and therefore all public employees should rigorously be excluded from any sales promotional personal incentive scheme; it should be made clear that either a specific discount is offered in lieu or that it is open to public authorities to negotiate their own terms.

2 Any promotional personal material incentive offered without the employer's knowledge to an employee to order goods or services or to make recommendations which result in such an order breaks the British Code of Sales Promotion – 'No trade incentive which is directed towards employees should be such as to cause any conflict with their duty to their employer' – because the employee is being induced to make decisions for his own personal gain rather than basing decisions upon proper commercial criteria, ie benefit for his employer.

The employer might wish to accept such offers in order to run a staff incentive scheme, buy goods for his business or pass on to the end consumer. However, it must be the employer's decision and he, ie in a company the chief executive or his delegated nominee, must be informed of the proposed offer. Documentation recording the supply of such offers should be forwarded to any recipient company.

3 Where promotional offers are 'trade related' or more simply the 'baker's dozen' it should be made clear that such offers are for the use of the organisation receiving the goods and they should be shown on advice notes and invoices.

4 Sales promotional offers or personal incentives should never be sent to businesses who have informed a supplier that it is against their policy to entertain such offers.

5 The *occasional* mailing mistakes may occur and in order to safeguard the promoting company and the recipient every printed trade promotion based on personal material incentive schemes should prominently display the following form of words:

> This promotional incentive scheme is not open to any Government Department or Public Authority.
> It is our policy to ensure that the management of every business receiving this promotion is fully aware of its terms and it is only profferred on the understanding that this scheme has the endorsement of the management, ie the chief executive or his/her nominee. As an extra precaution employees should ensure that this scheme has received such an endorsement.

Appendix 8

CHECKLIST OF RESTRICTIONS ON SALES PROMOTION ACTIVITIES IN INDIVIDUAL COUNTRIES

Published by, and reproduced here with permission of, IMP Europe, 197 Knightsbridge, London SW77 1RP, Tel: 0171–581 7666; Fax: 0171–589 3903.

One Law? – No?

	UK	Irish Republic	Spain	West Germany	France	Denmark	Belgium	Nether-lands
On-pack price reductions	●	●	●	●	●	●	●	●
Banded offers	●	●	●	▲	●	▲	▲	●
In-pack premiums	●	●	●	▲	▲	▲	▲	▲
Multi-purchase offers	●	●	●	▲	●	▲	▲	●
Extra product	●	●	●	▲	●	●	▲	▲
Free product	●	●	●	●	●	●	▲	●
Reusable/alternative use pack	●	●	●	●	●	●	●	●
Free mail-ins	●	●	●	○	●	▲	▲	●
With-purchase premiums	●	●	●	▲	●	▲	▲	▲
Cross-product offers	●	●	●	○	●	▲	○	▲
Collector devices	●	●	●	○	▲	▲	▲	▲
Competitions	●	●	●	▲	▲	▲	●	▲
Self-liquidating premiums	●	●	●	●	●	●	●	▲
Free draws	●	●	●	○	●	○	○	○
Share-outs	●	●	●	○	▲	○	○	○
Sweepstake/lottery	▲	▲	▲	▲	▲	○	▲	▲
Money-off vouchers	●	●	●	○	●	▲	●	●
Money-off next purchase	●	●	●	○	●	○	●	●
Cash backs	●	●	●	▲	●	●	●	●
In-store demos	●	●	●	●	●	●	●	●

Note This checklist is only a general guide. Professional advice should be sought in individual cases.

As with every aspect of its day-to-day life, each European nation has its own laws in relation to Sales, Marketing and Advertising. It is this complex legal diversity that makes the appointment of a genuine European agency network even more vitally important to the International marketeer.

Portugal	Italy	Greece	Luxembourg	Austria	Finland	Norway	Sweden	Switzerland
●	●	●	●	●	●	●	●	●
●	●	●	○	▲	▲	▲	▲	○
●	●	●	○	▲	●	▲	▲	○
●	●	●	○	▲	▲	▲	▲	○
●	●	●	●	▲	●	●	▲	▲
●	●	●	●	●	●	●	●	●
●	●	●	●	▲	●	●	●	●
●	●	●	▲	○	●	▲	○	○
●	●	●	○	▲	●	▲	▲	○
●	●	●	○	▲	▲	▲	▲	○
●	●	●	○	○	▲	○	○	○
●	●	●	▲	▲	●	●	●	●
●	●	●	○	●	●	○	●	○
●	●	●	○	○	●	○	○	○
●	▲	●	○	○	▲	▲	○	○
▲	▲	▲	○	▲	●	○	○	○
●	▲	●	▲	▲	▲	○	▲	○
●	▲	●	○	○	▲	○	○	○
●	○	●	○	▲	▲	▲	●	○
●	●	●	●	●	●	●	●	●

● *permitted* ○ *not permitted* ▲ *may be permitted*

Appendix 9
USEFUL ADDRESSES

Advertising Standards Authority
(and Committee of Advertising Practice)
Brook House, Torrington Place, London WC1E 7HN
0171-580 5555

Advertising Standards Board of Finance Ltd
Bloomsbury House, 74-77 Great Russell Street, London WC1B 3DA
0171-580 7071

Broadcast Advertising Clearance Centre
200 Gray's Inn Road, London WC1X 8HF
0171-843 8265

Cinema Advertising Association
127 Wardour Street, London W1V 4AD
0171- 439 9531

Data Protection Registrar
Wycliffe House, Water Lane, Wilmslow, Cheshire SK9 5AF
01625-535777 (Enquiries); 01625-535711 (Administration)

Direct Marketing Association (UK)
Haymarket House, 1 Oxendon Street, London SW1Y 4EE
0171-321 2525

European Commission (London Office)
Jean Monnet House, 8 Storey's Gate, London SW1P 3AT
0171-973 1992

Incorporated Society of British Advertisers
44 Hertford Street, London W1Y 8AE
0171-499 7502

Independent Committee for the Supervision of
Standards of Telephone Information Services
3rd Floor, Kingsbourne House, 229–231 High Holborn,
London WC1V 7DA
0171–430 2228

Independent Television Commission
33 Foley Street, London W1P 7LB
0171–255 3000

Institute of Practitioners in Advertising
44 Belgrave Square, London SW1X 8QS
0171–235 7020

Chartered Institute of Purchasing and Supply
Easton House, Easton on the Hill, Stamford, Lincs PE9 3NZ
01780– 56777

Institute of Sales Promotion
Arena House, 66–68 Pentonville Road, Islington,
London N1 9HS
0171–837 5340

Institute of Trading Standards Administration
Units 4 and 5, Hadleigh Business Centre, 351 London Road,
Hadleigh, Essex SS7 2BT
01702 559922

Local Authorities Coordinating Body on Food and Trading
Standards (LACOTS)
PO Box 6, Robert Street, Croydon CR9 1LG
0181–688 1996

Mail Order Protection Scheme
16 Tooks Court, London EC4A 1LB
0171–405 6806

Mailing Preference Service
5 Reef House, Plantation Wharf, London SW11 3UF
0171–738 1625

Office of Fair Trading
Field House, Breams Buildings, London EC4A 1PR
0171-242 2858

Radio Authority
Holbrook House, 14 Great Queen Street, London WC2 5DG
0171-430 2724

Telephone Preference Service
6 Reef House, Plantation Wharf, London SW11 3UF
0171-738 9053

INDEX

Accommodation
  free, 69
  holiday. *See* HOLIDAY
  price indication, 51, 171, *see also* PRICE INDICATION
Additional quantity packs, 70–73
Addresses, 222–224
Administration, 105–109
  Sales Promotion Code, rules, 130–131
Advertisement, *see also* ADVERTISING CODE, ADVERTISING STANDARDS AUTHORITY, COMMITTEE OF ADVERTISING PRACTICE
  child, addressed to, 137–139
  cigarettes, for. *See* CIGARETTES
  comparative advertising, and trade mark infringement, 48
  consumer credit control, 89–90
  decency, 118, 120
  employment, for, 151–153
  Europe, co-ordination in, 103–104
  honesty, 118, 120
  information in, where goods not seen, 92–93
  legality, 118, 120
  legislation affecting, 158–160, 164
  mail order, 23
  misleading, 8, 167
  motoring, 140
  newspaper, 64, 116, 187
  political, 121–122, 126
  prerogative of media owner, 165
  price indication in, 64
  private, 116
  promotion, Sales Promotion Code rules, 134
  self-regulatory system for, 5–10, 160–161, 163–167
    funding of, 165
    sanctions, 167
  television and radio, 10
  trade promotion guidance, 83, 211–213
  truthfulness, 118, 120
Advertiser. *See* PROMOTER
Advertising Code, 6, 118–126, 136–167, *see also* specific entries
  alcohol, 121, *see also* ALCOHOLIC DRINK
  application of, 116–118
  confusion not to be caused, 125, 126
  definitions in, 117
  delivery, postage, etc, costs, 124
  denigration, 125
  documentary evidence, 119, 167
  endorsements, 123
  fear, use of, 121
  free offer, 123–124
  goodwill to others, 125
  guarantee, 124–125
  identity of advertiser, 126
  indivisibility, 118
  legal, decent, honest and truthful principle, 118, 120
  opinion, use of, 120–121
  price, 123
  principles, 118–119
  privacy, protection of, 122
  product availability, 124
  resemblance to other advert, 125
  testimonials, 122–123
  unsafe practices, 121
  violence, 121
Advertising Standards Authority, 5–6
  appeal against adjudication of, 166
  case reports, 7
  Cigarette Code, role as to, 154
  complaint investigation, 162–163, 165–167
  delay in responding to enquiries, 119, 127
  interpretation of Codes, 117
  role of, 162–163
  Secretariat, 163, 166
Ageing, claims of delay to, 142, 144

Agents, use of, 163–164, 188–189, see also EMPLOYMENT AGENT, HANDLING HOUSE, TRAVEL COMPANY
Agreement. See CONTRACT
Air miles vouchers, 87–88
Alcoholic drink, 10, 121, 129, 136–137
  children, and, 121, 129, 136
  low alcohol drink, 137
  meaning, 136
Ancillary charges, 63, 67
Appeal, 2, 3
Application form, 206–208, see also CONTRACT, COUPON
Arbitration, 2
Auction, mock, 93
Audit
  handling house, by, 205
Austria, 221
Availability of goods, 62, 124, 129
  handling house, and, 203–204
  limited, and price indication, 183

Baldness, 145
Bar code, 194, 195
Beauty product or therapy
  restrictions on, 141–142, 144–145
  substantiation of claims, 141
Belgium, 220
Benelux countries, 102, 220
Book, 117, 119
Book club, 77
Bribery and corruption, 3, 80 et seq
  employee, incentive to, and conflict of interests, 82-3, 84, 212
  meaning of bribery, 81
  Note on trade incentives, 211–213
  penalties, 84
  prosecution for, 84
  public servant, bribe, gift, etc, to, 81–82, see also PUBLIC SERVANT
  trade incentives and business gifts, 82, 84–85
Briefings, 107
British Code of Advertising Practice. See ADVERTISING CODE
British Code of Sales Promotion Practice. See SALES PROMOTION CODE
Broadcast Advertising Clearance Centre, 10
Brochure, 188, see also MAIL ORDER GOODS

Budgeting, 107
Building work, VAT on, 184
Business, see also TRADE PROMOTION
  gifts. See GIFT
  hospitality, 215–216
  opportunity, offer of, 152

CAP. See COMMITTEE OF ADVERTISING PRACTICE
Call-out charge, 186
Care and skill, 19
Case law, 3, 7
Cash, 65, see also PAYMENT
  trade incentive, for, 213
Catalogue, see also MAIL ORDER GOODS
  price indications, 188
  price reduction rules for, 54, 176
Charity
  lottery for, 27
  promotions, 93–95, 134–135
Chartered Institute of Purchasing and Supply
  Ethical Code, 214–216
    binding institute members, 214
    breach, 214
  trade promotions, Code, 83, 217–218
Checklist, 105–109
  development of promoter's own, 109
  handling house, for, 209–210
Children, 20, 75–76, 121, 129, 137–139
  alcohol or tobacco advertising, 121, 129, 136, 157
  charitable promotion, and 135
  distance selling packaging, and, 149
  rules for advert or promotion addressed to, 137–139
  vitamins and minerals, 144
Cigar, 155
Cigarettes, 116, 117, 129
  Code on, 154–158
    clearance of advert for, 156
    coupon brands, 157
    principles, 156
    rules, 156–158
    sports sponsorship, 154, 155, 158
  Committee for Monitoring Agreements on Tobacco Advertising and Sponsorship, 154

Cinema
   commercial, 116, *see also* ADVERTISEMENT
   tickets, 186
Civil law, 1–2
Claims
   documentary evidence to support, 119, 167
Closing date
   children, need for prominence for, 139
   coupon, for use of, 193
   free offer, for, 68
   introductory offer, for, 57
   prize promotion, for, 132
   Sales Promotion Code rule, 130
Clothes, 92–93
Codes of Practice, 4–10, *see also* ADVERTISING CODE, SALES PROMOTION CODE, ETC
   breaches, 7, 119, 127
   categories of, 4
   complementary role, 164
   self–regulatory system, 5–10, 160–161, 163–167
      funding, 165
      publicity and other sanctions, 7, 167
   statutory codes, 4–5, 7–8
Commercials, 116, *see also* ADVERTISEMENT
Committee of Advertising Practice, 6, 160
   advice on copy from, 8
   case reports, 7
   chairman, 161
   General Media Review Panel, 8, 162
   members, 114
   role, 161–162
   Secretariat, 163, 166
   working groups, use of, 162
Common law, 3–4
Communication
   effective, need for, 107
Company
   information about, on order form, 92
   trade incentives. *See* TRADE PROMOTION
   use of, as supplier, 22, 106
Comparisons, 58–60, 125, *see also* PRICE INDICATION
Compensation, 2

Competition, 33 *et seq*
   challenge to, dealing with, 108–109
   change to after commencement, 40
   closing date, 38, 39, 132, 133
      delay to, 40
   contract, as, 37–38, 40
   entries
      copyright, 39, 132
      response to, 131
      returning, 39, 132
   factorial, 36–37
   illegal, 33–35
      avoiding, 33–38
      forecasting events, 34–35
   judges, 133
   judging criteria, 39, 132
   meaning, 33
   payment, 35
   permissions for entry, 39, 40, 132
   prize
      cash alternative, 39, 41
      chance not to be exaggerated, 134, 139
      Code requirements, 132–134
      description of, 38, 40, 132
      highly unlikely to be won, 37
      product liability if defective, 38
      time for receipt of, 133
   proof of purchase, 38, 40, 132
   publicity, 41
   ranking, 36–37
   regular, 117
   restriction on entries, 38, 39, 40, 132
   rules
      contractual issues, 37–38
      failure to abide by, 40
      Sales Promotion Code, complying with, 38–40, 133
      shortening, 39–40
      supplementary, 39
   skill, need for, 33, 36
   'spot the ball', 36
   tie–breakers, 35
   types, 36–37
   winners
      notification of, 39, 40, 132
      publication of names, 133
      use of, post–event, 39, 41, 133
Complaints, 108, 162–163, 165–167
Computer, *see also* DATA PROTECTION, MAILING LIST
   information kept on, 74–75, 78–79

Computer game
    advertisement in, 116
Confidentiality, 44–45, 204, 208, 215
Conflict of interest, 127, 212, see also EMPLOYEE
    declaration of, 215
Consumer credit, 89–90
    advertising controls, 89–90
    credit linked promotions, 90
    enforcement of law on, 3
    offences, 90
Consumer protection, 3, 14, 164, see also CONTRACT, SAFETY OF GOODS
    European Community, in, 99, 103–104
    handling houses, and, 201, 202, 203–204
    legislation, 158–160
    price indications. See PRICE INDICATION
    Sales Promotion Code, 128–129
Contempt of court, 167
Contract, 11 et seq, 106–107
    acceptance, 11, 12
    application for incentive goods, as acceptance, 12
    clear and comprehensive, need for, 15, 106–107
    competition entry, for, 37
    consideration, 11
    delivery of incentive goods, 15
    disclaimer, 14–15
    express term, 12
    faulty goods, 16, 18–19
    fulfilment of promotional offer, 12–13, 16, 17
    illegal promotion, for, 204
    implied term, 12, 18–20
    information in, 15, 16–17, 19, 22
    intention to create legal relations, 11–12
    meaning, 11
    misdescription, 16–17
    offer and acceptance, 11
    offer terms, 12, 13, 15–16
        'equivalent value' alternative, 13
        expiry date, 13, 21
        extension of offer, 14
        limitations on offer, 13–14, 21
        wording requirements, 15
    promotion agreement as, 12
    quality of goods, 16, 18–19
    refunds, 16, 17
    rejection of goods, right, 19

Contract – *continued*
    services. See SERVICES
    single, for substantive and promotional products, 16
    suitability of goods, 20
    terms, 12
Copyright
    application to promotional material, 46–47
    assignment or licence, need for, 47
    automatic right, 43
    competition entry, rules to provide for, 39, 132
    compilations, 42–43
    duration, 43
    employee, work created as, 42, 46
    exclusions from protection, 42–43
    film, 43, 45, 46
    ideas, 42, 44–45
        confidence, imparted in, 44–45
        protection of, 44–45
    infringement, 49
    injunction, 49
    meaning, 42
    moral rights, 45–46
        agencies, and, 45–46
        derogatory treatment of work, objection to, 46
        identification as author, 45–46
        waiver, 45–46
    ownership, 43
    protection, steps for, 47
Corruption. See BRIBERY AND CORRUPTION
Cosmetics, 144–145
Coupon, 65–66, 86–88
    bar codes, 194–195
    cigarettes, for, 157
    closing dates, 193, 196
    Code on, 191–197
    design, 206–208
    free product, 196
    gathering scheme, 138
    handling allowance, 197
    incorporated into leaflet, etc, 194
    information on, 206–208
    instructions on, 195
    materials, 197
    money-off, 86, 87, 88, 95, 196
        differentiation from other offer, 196
    Notes for Guidance, 9, 66, 191–197
    on-pack, 195–196
        notification of traders, 196

Coupon – *continued*
'off next purchase', typeface, 193, 196
product details, 195
promoter's name and address on, 195
size and shape, 193
validity, statement of, 193
value, 193
wording, 193
Court
civil law matter, for, 2
criminal law case, 3
Cover charge, 184–185
Credit, 186
canvassing, offence, 90, *see also* CONSUMER CREDIT
Credit card
price differential for payment by, 65
Criminal law, 2–4, 17–18, 19
bribery and corruption prosecution, 84
consumer product safety liability, 89
illegal lottery prosecution, 31–32
Crossword, 117

Damage
goods causing. *See* SAFETY OF GOODS
goods suffering, 148, *see also* FAULTY GOODS
Dangerous or noxious items, 20, *see also* SAFETY OF GOODS
children not to be shown with, 138
handling house, procedure for, 206
mail order exclusion, 75
Data protection, 74–75, 78–79, 149–151, *see also* MAILING LIST
handling house, and, 204, 208–209
List and Database Practice, Specific Rules, 129
Decency, in advert, 118, 120
Delivery, of, 15, 209–210
charge for, 124, 131
foreign country, to, 149
'free' goods, and, 67
high value goods, 149
price indication, 63, 183
time for, 15, 147–148
Demand
anticipation of, 13, 107
Denmark, 102, 220
Deposit
offer of no, or low, 90

Description
incentive goods, of, 16–17
mail order goods, of, 75
prize, of, 38, 40, 132
Destruction of goods
handling house, by, 205–206
Direct response, 74 *et seq*, *see also* MAIL ORDER GOODS
advertiser, identity of, 126
information in, 23
Direct Marketing Association, 74
Director General of Fair Trading, 5
consumer credit advertising, recommendation, 90
powers as to misleading advertisements, etc, 8, 167
Disclaimer, 14–15
price reduction, and, 53
Distance selling, 74, 147–149
delivery, 147–148
information in advert, 147
payment, 148
refunds, 147, 148
withdrawal, 148
Distributor
liability for damage from product, 89
Drink, *see also* ALCOHOLIC DRINK
price indication, 176
Driving, *see also* MOTORING
alcohol, and, 121

Employee
gift or incentive to, conflict of interest, 82-3, 84, 211–213, 217–218
employer's consent and other safeguards, 83, 135
non–cash incentive prize, Inland Revenue approval, 94–95
public. *See* PUBLIC SERVANT
work created as, and copyright, 42, 46
Employment, offer of, 151–153
Employment agency, 152
Endorsements, 122–123, 157
Enforcement, 3, 164, 172
Environmental claims, 140, 141
Environmental health officer, 164
Estimates
demand, etc, of, need for, 107
Ethics, 214–216

European Advertising Standards Alliance, 103, 167
European Community, 96–97, 220–221
   advertising co-ordination, 103–104
   Cassis de Dijon case, 101
   Commission, 97–98
      Green Paper on Commercial Communications, 100
      involvement in marketing, 99–100
      consumer protection in, 99, 103–104
   Council of Ministers, 97
   Court of Justice, 98
   Directives, 100
   EC Treaty, 96–97
   Economic and Social Committee, 98–99
   European Parliament, 98
   free movement of goods, 101
      national restrictions, abandonment of, 101
   institutions, 97
   legislation, 100–101
   Regulations, 100–101
   sales promotion rules in other states, 102–103, 220–221
      obtaining advice on, 102–103
   self-regulation, 103–104, 167
European Free Trade Association, 103
European Union, 96, see also EUROPEAN COMMUNITY
   creation and meaning of, 96
Evidence, 119, 127, 167
Exercise programme, advert for, 146

Fair competition, 127
Fair trading. See DIRECTOR GENERAL OF FAIR TRADING
Faulty goods, 16, 131
Fee, professional, VAT on, 184
Finance, 186
   no deposit or low interest, 90
Financial services, 153–154
Fitting
   free offer of goods, advertiser to fit, 68–69
   offer as to, 68
Food
   labelling, 72
   pack sizes, 71–72

Food – *continued*
   pre-packed cheese, meat and milk, 65
   price indication, 176
Food substitutes, 146
Food supplements, 144
France, 102, 220
Free draw, 132
Free fitting, 19–20
Free movement of goods, 101
   foreign lottery, and, 32
Free offer, 67 *et seq*, 123–124, 131–132
   ancillary charges, 67, 182
   conditions, 67, 182
   coupon, 196
   extra pack, 72–73
   extra value packs, 70–73
   fitting, wording for, 68
   'free', use of, 67
   multiple packs, 72–73
   period of, 68
   petrol, wine, etc, 69
   price indication, 67, 182
   travel and accommodation, 69
   value, ascribing of, 69–70
Free samples, 20
Freelancer, 43, 46
Fulfilment of offer. *See* CONTRACT

Game of chance, *see also* LOTTERY
   linked to purchase of product, 25–27
Germany, 102, 220
Gift, 69, *see also* FREE OFFER
   business, 215–216, *see also* TRADE PROMOTION
      tax implications, 85
   distinguish from prize, need to, 134
   presumption of corruption, circumstances for, 81, *see also* BRIBERY AND CORRUPTION
   unsolicited goods as, 21, 76
Goodwill, exploitation of, 125
Greece, 220, 221
Green. *See* ENVIRONMENTAL CLAIMS
Guarantee, 124
   money-back, 132, 148

Hair product, 145
Handling costs, 67, 124, 131
   allowance to traders for coupons, 197

Handling house
  accounts, 205
  advertising of services, 204
  applications
    form, 206–208
    processing, 208
  audit, 205
  brief to, 202, 203, 208, 209–210
  checks on, 106
  Code on promotional handling, 9, 106, 198–210
    administration, 201
    adoption, effect of, 201
    definitions, 201
    principles, 202–206
    prompt list, 209–210
    recommendations, 206–209
  confidentiality, 204, 208
  consumer protection, 201, 202, 203–204
  data ownership, 204
  data protection, 208
  definition in Code, 201
  delay, 203
  destruction of products, 205–206
  errors and problems, 205
  illegal, etc, promotions, 204
  information
    accuracy warranty, 205
    application form or coupon, on, 206–208
  insufficient stock, 203–204
  Promotional Handling Association, 106
  quotation, 203
  relationship with client, 206
  return of goods, 206
  stock levels, 204
  use of, 22, 106
Health products, 141–145
Holiday, 185–186, see also TRAVEL COMPANY
  brochure, 188
  package, 69, 185
Home, new, price indication, 171, 189–190
Homework scheme, 152
Honesty
  advert, in, 118, 120
  sales promotion, 127, 128
Hospitality, business, 215
Hotel, service charges, 184–185

ICSTIS, 9, 116
ITC, 10
Illegal competition, 33–35
  avoiding running, 33–38
  forecasting events, 34–35
Illegal lottery, 31–32
Illegal promotion
  handling house withdrawal, 204
Incentive product
  describing. See ADVERTISEMENT, DESCRIPTION, INFORMATION
  trade incentives, 84–84, 135, 211–213, see also BRIBERY AND CORRUPTION, TRADE PROMOTION
  unsolicited. See UNSOLICITED GOODS
Incorporated Society of British Advertisers
  guidance on trade promotions, 83, 211–213
Independent Committee for the Supervision of Standards of Telephone Information Services, 9, 116
Independent Television Commission, 10
  Code, 10
Information, see also ADVERTISEMENT
  accuracy, 205, 215, see also PRICE INDICATION
  application form, on, 206–208
  charitable promotion, required for, 94
  children, for, 75–76
  clarity requirement, 15, 16–17, 19
  computer, kept on, 74–75, 78–79, 149–151
  distance selling advert, in, 147
  handling house warranty, 205
  identity of contracting party, 22–23
  labelling, 70, 72–73, 91, see also PRICE INDICATION
  lists. See MAILING LIST
  order forms, on, 92
  participation in promotion, as to, 130
  quantity, as to, 70, 72
Injunction
  advertisement or promotion, to prevent, 167
  infringement of copyright etc, to prevent, 49
Inland Revenue. See TAX

'Instant win', 28–30, 45, 132, 133–134
Institute of Sales Promotion, 9
   administration of Promotional Handling Code of Practice, 201
Insurance, 186, 188
   holiday, 185
Intellectual property, 42 *et seq*, *see also* COPYRIGHT, PATENT, TRADE MARK
   meaning, 42
Interest
   offer of low, regulation of, 90
   rates, basis for calculation of, 153
International Chamber of Commerce, Codes, 103
Introductory offer, 57–58, 177, *see also* PRICE INDICATION
Investment opportunity, 152, 153
Ireland, 102, 220
Italy, 220, 221

Label gathering scheme, 138
Labelling, 70, 72–73, *see also* PRICE INDICATION
   Codes, application of, 117
   origin of goods, indication of, 91
   textile products, on, 92–93
Leaflet, 188, *see also* MAIL ORDER GOODS
   coupon incorporated into, 194
Legality, *see also* ILLEGAL entries
   advert, of, 118, 120
   sales promotion, of, 127, 128
Liability, *see also* PRODUCT LIABILITY
   limitation of, 14
Limited edition, 21
List. *See* MAILING LIST
Local Authorities Co–ordinating Body on Food and Trading Standards, 3
Lottery, 24 *et seq*
   avoiding running
      free game, 25–26, 28, 29
      no expectation of chance, 26
      non–purchase and on–pack compared, 29–30
      proceeds to charity, 27
      skill, need for, 31, *see also* COMPETITION
   contribution towards, 25–27, 30–31
      participant, by, 25
      payment to get prize distinguished, 32

Lottery – *continued*
      telephone call or stamp, whether is, 30–31
      trade promotions, 26–27
      what constitutes, 30–31
   enforcement of law on, 3
   foreign, 31–32
   game of chance, as, 25
      participation in dependent on action by participant, 30
   illegal, liability for, 31–32
   knowledge that is, 26
   meaning, 24–25
   newspaper bingo, 28
   no obligation visit, test drive, etc, 30
   payment, *see* 'contribution towards' above
   prize
      discount as, 32
      free prize draw rules, 32
      need for, 25
   questionnaire, filling in, 30
   restrictions on, 24, 130
   scratch card scheme, 28–30
Luxembourg, 102, 220, 221

Maastricht Treaty, 96
Magazine
   advertisement of goods in, price, 64, 187, *see also* ADVERTISEMENT
   Advertising Code, application to, 116
   coupon incorporated into, 194
Mail order goods, 64, 74 *et seq*
   advertiser, identity of, 126
   children, and, 139
   clothes, information in advertisement, 92–93
   controls for, 74–76
   description, 75
   distance selling, 74, *see also* DISTANCE SELLING
   fair trading standards, 74
   goods which cannot be sold, 75
   hoax order, 77–78
   identity of trader, 22–23, 67
   incorrect details, 77–78
   mailing lists. *See* MAILING LIST
   post and packing charges, 63
   price indication rules, 64, 176, 188
   price reduction rules for, 54
   standard of goods, 75

Mail order goods – *continued*
unsolicited promotional goods. *See* UNSOLICITED GOODS
Mailing list, 74–75, 78–79
accuracy, 149
appropriateness of people mailed, 150
collection of information for, 150–151
consumer's rights, 150–151
controls, 74–75, 78–79, 116, 149–151
copying, 79
dead person, 78, 149
disclosure, 149, 150
errors, 78
MPS Suppression File, 149, 151
owner, 149, 150
restrictions on use, 78–79
up–to–date, need to be, 149, 150
user, 149, 150
Mailing Preference Service, 149, 151
Marketing
sales promotion as part of, 105–106
Medicine, 10, 138, 142–144
homeopathic, 143
prescription only, 143
Minerals, 144, 146
Misdescription, 16–17
Misleading
advertisement, 8, 167
price indication
becoming, after given, 187–189
defence, 172
definition, 171
offence, 51 *et seq*, 171 *et seq*
Mock auction, 93
Moral rights, 45–46
Motoring, 140
alcohol, and, 121
price, 140
safety and environmental claims, 140

Netherlands, 220, 221
Newspaper
advertisement of goods in, price, 64, 187, *see also* ADVERTISEMENT
Advertising Code, application to, 116
bingo, 28
Nightwear, flammability notice, 93
Non–receipt of goods, 131, 148

Obscenity, 20, 75, *see also* DECENCY, SEXUAL TECHNIQUES
Offer. *See* CONTRACT
Office of Fair Trading. *See* DIRECTOR GENERAL OF FAIR TRADING
On–pack
coupon, 195–196
lottery, 29–30
Order, 206–207, *see also* CONTRACT, COUPON
hoax, 87–88
Order form, 92
Origin of goods, indication of, 91
Own–brand goods
liability for damage to consumer, 89
price indication, 59

Packaging, 117, 164
Packing. *See* HANDLING, POST AND PACKING COSTS
Packs
banding of, 71, 72–73
multiple, one free, 72–73
size, 71–72
Patent, 42, 49–50
meaning, 49
relevance to sales promotion, 50
Payment, 21, 22–23
cash, 65, 213
competition, for entry to, 35
contribution to, in lottery, 25
credit card, 65
distance selling, information on, 148
Sales Promotion Code rules, 131
unsolicited goods, 76
Penalties, 167, *see also* COMPLAINTS
Perishable goods, 147, 149, 176
Permission, 130, 132
children, and promotion for, 76, 138
entry to competition, for, 39, 40
Personal visit, 149
Pipe, 155
Place of production, indication of, 91
Political advertising, 121–122, 126
Portugal, 220, 221
Post and packing costs, 63, 67, 124, 131, 183
Postcode, use of, 208
Pregnant woman
vitamins and minerals, 144
Price indication, 51 *et seq*
advertisement, in, 64, 123

Price indication – *continued*
  'after–promotion price', use of, 58, 177–178
  ancillary charges, 63
  availability of goods, and, 62
  call–out charges, 186
  charging higher price than marked, 51–52, 182
  Code, 51, 168–190
    definitions, 173–174
    effect of following, 172–173
    'price', 173
    scope, 171
  comparisons, 58–60, 125, 171–172, 174–182
    dangers associated with, 59–60
    different circumstances. *See* 'Different circumstances comparisons', below
    general statements as to other prices, 59, 180
    initials, use of, 55, 175, 177
    other trader's prices, with, 58–60, 179–180
    price promise statement, 59
    range of goods, guidance for, 60
    RRP, etc, with, 55–57, 180–181
    rules, 58–59, 174 *et seq*
    trader's own previous price, with, 52–54, 175–176
  coupons, 65–66
  credit facilities, 186
  delivery. *See* DELIVERY
  different circumstances comparisons, 61–62, 178–179
    different condition, 62, 178–179
    different people, 62–63, 179
    different quantities, 61–62, 178
    kit or ready–assembled, 62, 179
    special order, 62
  different prices, indicating, 51–52, 182
  due diligence defence, 172–173
  enforcement of law on, 3, 172
  flash offer, goods marked with, 57, 181
  food, 176
  'free' goods, 67, 182, *see also* FREE OFFER
  future price, 58, 177–178
  guidance on, 168–190
  holidays. *See* HOLIDAY

Price indication – *continued*
  home, sale of new, 171, 189–190
  insurance, 185, 186, 188
  introductory offer, 57–58, 177
    extension of period, 58
    period for, 57
  kits, 62, 179, 183
  legislation, 173
  less than real price, 51–52
  limited availability, 183
  limited period, 187
  mail order goods. *See* MAIL ORDER GOODS
  misleading
    becoming, after given, 187–189
    defence, 172
    definition, 171
    offence, 51 *et seq*, 171 *et seq*
  newspaper, etc, in. *See* NEWSPAPER, MAGAZINE
  own–brand, 59
  post and packing, 63, 67, 183
  pre–packed goods, 65
  recommended prices, comparison with, 55–57, 180–181
    selling below manufacturer's marked price, 56
  reductions, 52–55, 60–63, 175–177
    disclaimer, 53
    positive statement as to, 53–54
    previous price indication, restrictions on, 54–55, 62–63
    rules for indicating, 52–53
    series, on same goods, 54, 177
  resale price maintenance, 56
  sales, 60–61, 181–182
  seconds, 62
  service charges, etc, 184–185
  special events, 60–61, 181–182
  tickets, face value, 186
  unit price, requirement for, 64–65
  value added tax, 63, 183–184
    change in rate, 189
  value or worth, statement as to, 60, 181
  vouchers, 65–66
Privacy, protection of, 122
Prize. *See* COMPETITION, LOTTERY, PRIZE PROMOTION
Prize promotion, 132–134, *see also* COMPETITION, LOTTERY
  cash alternative, 132
  children, and, 76

children, and, 76
Prize promotion – *continued*
  closing date, 132, 133
  employee, to, 94–95
  fairness, 133
  judges, 133
  notification of winners, 132
  prize
    distinguish from gift, need to, 134
    exaggeration of chance of, 134, 139
    nature of, information on, 132
    time for receipt of, 133
  restrictions and permissions, 132
  rules, Sales Promotion Code on, 38–40, 129
Producer
  liability for damage from product, 89
Product liability, 38, 89
Promoter
  charitable, 94
  checklist for, 105–109
  development of own, 109
  corruption, prosecution for, 80–81, 84, *see also* CRIMINAL LAW
  duties. *See* SALES PROMOTION CODE
  identity of, 22–23, 66, 74, 126, 130, 147
    coupon, on, 195
  protection of, 128–129
  responsibility of, 163
  use of supplier, 106
Proof of purchase, 130, 209, 210
  children, and explanation of, 76
  competition, for, 38, 40
Promotional handling. *See* HANDLING HOUSE
Public figures, 122, 143, *see also* TESTIMONIAL
Public interest, 127
Public servant
  bribe, gift, etc, made to member, 81–82, 211–213, 217
  prosecution for, penalties, 84
Purchasing and supply, Institute of.
  See CHARTERED INSTITUTE OF PURCHASING AND SUPPLY
Purchasing officer, 82, 84–85

Quality, 16, 18–19, 19–20
  outside supplier, standard, 106

Quantity, indication of, 70, 72
  extra quantity packs, 70–73

Radio, 10
Radio Authority, 10
Record club, 77
Records, need for, 108–109, 213
Reduction in price, 52–55, 60–63, 175–177
  disclaimer, 53
  positive statement as to, 53–54
  previous price indication, restrictions on, 54–55, 62–63
Refunds, 16, 17, 131, 132
  distance selling, and, 147, 148–149
Restaurant, service charges, 184–185
Return of goods, 147, 148, *see also* FAULTY GOODS
  handling house, by, 206
  rejection, right of, 19
Royal Family, reference to, 122

Safety of goods, 88–89
  general safety requirement, 88, 89
  goods offered free, control of, 88
  liability, 38, 89
    strict, 88
  own–label goods, 89
Sale goods, 60–61, 181–182
Sales Promotion Code, 6–7, 107, 126–135, 136–167, *see also* specific entries
  administration, 130–131
  advertisement promotion, 134
  alcohol, 129
  application of, 116–118, 126
  cigarettes, 129
  closing date, 130
  consumer, protection of, 128–129
  definitions in, 117
  employee, incentive to, guidance, 84
  entries, responding to, 131
  fair competition, 127
  indivisibility, 118
  legislation affecting, 158–160, 164
  participation, information as to, 130
  payment, 131–132
  principles, 127
  product availability, 129
  promoter, protection of, 128–129
  proof of purchase, 130
  refunds, 131

Sales Promotion Code – *continued*
  scope, 7
  unsuitable or inappropriate material, 129
Sales promotion law
  civil law, 1–2
  criminal law, 2–4
  meaning, 1
  self–regulatory system, 5–10, 160–161, 163–167
    funding of, 165
    sanctions, 167
Scalp products, 145
Scientific expression, 141, 142
Scratch card promotion, 28
Sealskin goods, information on, 93
Secretariat (for ASA and CAP), 163, 166
Service charge, and price indication, 185
Services
  free, 67 et seq
  offer, with incentive, 12, 17
  payment for, as 'contribution', 25
  price indication, 51, 171, *see also* PRICE INDICATION
  quality, 19–20
  unsolicited, 20–21
Servicing of goods, 19
Sexual techniques, 20, 21, 77
Shape
  trade mark protection, 47
Slimming, 145
Slogans, 42, 47
Small claim, 2
Smell
  trade mark protection, 47
Smoking. *See* CIGARETTES
Sound
  trade mark protection, 47
Sourcing company, use of, 106
Spain, 220
Sport
  sponsorship, 154, 155, 158
  tickets for, 186
'Spot the ball' competition, 36
Stamp. *See* TRADING STAMP
Statutes, 3, 100–101, 158–160, 164, 173
Stock levels, 204
Substantiation, 119, 127
Suitability, 20
Summary offence, 3

Supplier
  quality control of, 106
Sweden, 221
Switch selling, 124
Switzerland, 221

Tax, 94–95
  trade incentive scheme or business gift, on, 85, 213
Telephones, 9, 116, 117
Television, 10, 116, *see also* ADVERTISEMENT
Testimonial, 122–123, 145
  smoking, and, 157
Textiles, 92–93
Tickets, 186
Time share, 69
Timetabling, 107
Third party, check on promotional material by, 109
Tobacco, hand–rolling, 154, 155, *see also* CIGARETTES
Token, 86, *see also* TRADING STAMP
Trade descriptions, 16, 17, 19, *see also* DESCRIPTION
Trade mark, 42, 47–49
  comparative advertising, 48
  criminal offence, 49
  infringement, 49
  injunction, 49
  registration, 47, 49
  scope of protection, 47
  search, 49
  use of, authorised, 48
Trade promotions
  conflict of interest, avoiding, 82–3, 84–85, 211–216
  guidance on, 83, 211–213, 217–218
  incentive scheme, 84–85, 135, 211–213
  lottery, whether is, 26–27
  purchasing officer, and, 82, 84–85
  Rules, 9, 217–218
  Sales Promotion Code guidance on, 84
  tax on trade incentive or business gift, 85, 135
Trading list. *See* MAILING LIST
Trading stamp, 86–88
  air miles vouchers, 87–88
  cash redemption value, 87, 88
  definition, 86

Trading stamps – *continued*
  money–off coupon, 86, 87, 88
    VAT, and, 95
  requirements, 87
Trading standards officer, 3, 164, 172
  obstructing, offence, 172
Training, offer of, 152–153
Travel
  cost of, 124, 131
  free, offer of, 69
  price indication, 69, 185–186
Travel company
  use of, 22, 106, 188
Truthfulness
  advert, in, 118, 120
  sales promotion, 127, 128
'Try me free' offer, 132

Unsolicited goods/services, 20–21, 76–78
  goods sent after cancellation of subscription, 77
  goods which may not be sent, 77
  meaning, 76
  payment, 76
Unwanted goods, 147, 148
  rejection, right of, 19

Value
  coupon, sterling value on, 193
  extra value incentives, 70–73, *see also* FREE OFFER
  'face value' of tickets, 186
  statement concerning, 60, 69–70
Value added tax
  distance selling advert, and, 147
  money–off coupon, and, 95
  price indication, 63, 183–184
    business customers, 184
    changes in rate, 189
    professional fees, 184
Vehicle. *See* MOTORING
Video commercial, 116, *see also* ADVERTISEMENT
Viewdata services, 116
Violence, 121
Vitamins, 144, 146
Voucher, 65–66, 86, *see also* COUPON, TRADING STAMP
  trade incentive, use for, 213

Wrapper gathering scheme, 138